GET THROUGH
LIFE IN THE UK TEST
1000 PRACTICE QUESTIONS
2013

Includes Major British Historical Events by Years in Tabulated Form

In line with the 3rd Edition of the Home Office Handbook

For Tests after 25th March 2013

SAMIRA YAHYA

D0524818

Authors:	Samira Yahya
	Azeem S Sheikh
First Edition:	April 2013

ISBN: 978-0-9574453-3-8

British Library Cataloguing in Publication Data.

A catalogue record for this book is available from the British Library.

Published & Distributed in the UK, by: Gold Beans
Gold Beans Publishing Ltd
5, Jupiter House
Calleva Park, Aldermaston
Reading
RG7 8NN

'Gold Beans' is a trading name for Gold Beans Publishing Ltd.

Place Orders @:
Contact No. :   (+44) 07956 829 786
Email for Orders: GoldBeansPublishing@gmail.com

Printed in the United Kingdom

Introduction

'Get Through Life In The UK Test, 1000 Practice Questions, 2013' is a study aid for people appearing in the Life in the UK Test, prior to applying for British Citizenship. The book contains questions, chapter by chapter, from the new [3rd Edition of the] official home office book 'Life in the United Kingdom -A Guide for New Residents' 3rd Edition.

The book has been developed to aid you to check your understanding of the official handbook chapters, by trying to attempt questions as you go on reading. It helps test your knowledge right during preparation rather than having to wait until you have read the entire book. This enables you to focus more, right there, when you are going through a chapter, if you find you are unable to answer the relevant questions correctly.

Please remember that these are **NOT the official test questions**. These are the questions we have developed with an intent to cover most of the substance of the official handbook. Since it's a huge compilation of questions, it is likely to provide an intense preparation opportunity. We hope if you practice all these before you apply for the test and are able to answer these fluently before you appear in the test, you will find the test very easy to navigate. The answers are given at the end of each practice test. If you find any of your answers do not match with the ones in our Answer Key, you can see the handbook page references in column 4 of the Answer Key and mark the relevant pages or chapters for a revised reading. Four mock tests in the end will help you in additional self-assessment of yourself once you have read all the chapters of the official handbook.

We strongly recommend to all prospective candidates to read the latest official home office book 'Life in the United Kingdom -A Guide for New Residents' 3rd Edition, [this one is the latest as per April 2013; you should check the latest information prior to your test].

Disclaimer:

Whilst the authors have endeavoured to prepare a good study aid, and the information provided here is believed to be correct at the time of publication, the authors cannot provide any guarantees of the factual accuracy or completeness of substance. We have taken immense care in preparing this study aid, but, the content of test material may keep changing and updating, and authors and publishers accept no responsibility for any errors or omissions or for the relevance of the material at any point in time. It is your own responsibility to ensure that you have up to date knowledge of relevant issues and test material from the official resources.

We do not accept any liability for any loss, damage, expense, costs or liability whatsoever incurred by you by use of our book.

We dedicate this book to our beloved parents whose love and care nurtured us to what we are today.

Acknowledgements:

Special Thanks to Abdullah Johar, Abdur Rehman, Roha, Maria, Shehzal and Ayesha for their unending love & support!

CONTENTS

	Page#
Section I	
Major Historical Events by Years	3
Section II	25
Chapter wise Practice Questions	
Chapter 1: The Values & Principles of the UK	
&	
Chapter 2: What is the UK?	
Practice Test	25
Answer Key	34
Chapter 3: A Long & Illustrious History	
Practice Test	37
Answer Key	115
Chapter 4: A Modern Thriving Society	
Practice Test	131
Answer Key	191

Chapter 5: The UK Government, the Law & Your Role

Practice Test   203

Answer Key   272

MOCK TESTS

Mock Test 1   287

Answer Key   294

Mock Test 2   295

Answer Key   302

Mock Test 3   303

Answer Key   310

Mock Test 4   311

Answer Key   318

Section 1

Major British Historical Events by Years

Year/ Period	Significant Events	Handbook Page No:
Stone Age	First people to live in Britain were hunter-gatherers, in what we call the Stone Age.	p.15
10,000 years ago	Britain only became permanently separated from the continent by the Channel about 10,000 years ago.	p.15
6000 years ago	The first farmers arrived in Britain 6000 years ago.	p.15
4000 years ago	Bronze Age [people learned to make bronze].	p.16
Iron Age	People learned how to make weapons and tools out of iron; first coins were minted.	p.16
55 BC	Julius Caesar led a Roman invasion of Britain.	p.17
AD 43	Emperor Claudius led the roman army in a new invasion.	p.17
3rd & 4th centuries AD	Christian communities began to appear in Britain.	p.17
AD 410	The Roman army left Britain to defend other parts of the Roman Empire.	p.17
AD 600	Anglo-Saxon Kingdoms were established in Britain.	p.17
After 600 AD	Saints & Missionaries came to preach in Britain.	p.18

Year/ Period	Significant Events	Handbook Page No:
AD 789	The Vikings came from Denmark and Norway.	p.19
AD 1066	An invasion led by William the conqueror, the Duke of Normandy (which is now in northern France)	p.19
AD 1066	Battle of Hastings [Same as above; that is, the invasion by William]	p.19
AD 1066	The Norman Conquest [Same as above, the conquest by William]	p.20
1066	The Tower of London was first built by William the Conqueror after he became king in 1066.	p.115
1066 to 1485	Middle Ages or Medieval Period [The period after the Norman conquest to 1485]	p.21
1284	King Edward I of England introduced the Statute of Rhuddlan, which annexed Wales to the crown of England.	p.21
1314	The Scottish, led by Robert the Bruce, defeated the English at the Battle of Bannockburn, and Scotland remained unconquered by the English.	p.21
1314	Battle of Bannockburn [Same as above]	p.21
1200	By 1200, the English ruled an area of Ireland known as the Pale, around Dublin.	p.21

Year/ Period	Significant Events	Handbook Page No:
Middle Ages	Crusades were fought, in which European Christians fought for control of the Holy land.	p.21
Middle Ages	100 years War with France, ending in 1415	p.21
1415	Battle of Agincourt [King Henry V defeated the French.] and that was the end of 100 Year War	p.21
1450	The English left France, at the end of the 100 years war.	p.21
1348	The Black Death - a form of plague, killed a third of population in UK	p.22
1215	King John was forced to agree to a charter of rights called the Magna Carta, that restricted the power of kings.	p.22
1400	English had become the preferred language of the royal court and the parliament.	p.23
1455--1485	War of Roses, a civil war in England to decide who will be the king, fought between Houses of Lancaster and York	p.25
1485	Battle of Bosworth, the deciding battle in War of Roses, when Henry Tudor from House of Lancaster won and became King Henry VII of England.	p.25
1530	Church of England was formed. [By Henry VIII]	p.26

Year/ Period	Significant Events	Handbook Page No:
1530	Reformation Act of 1530 [relating to formation of Church of England, as above].	p.77
1560	The Protestant Scottish Parliament abolished the authority of the Pope in Scotland. Roman Catholic religious services became illegal in Scotland.	p.29
1564	William Shakespeare (1564-1616)	p.30
1603	Elizabeth I died, her cousin James became King James I of England.	p.31
1605	On 5th November 1605, when a group of Catholics led by Guy Fawkes failed in their plan to kill the Protestant king with a bomb in the Houses of Parliament.	p.83
1642	Civil war between the King Charles I and parliament began in 1642.	p.33
1643	Isaac Newton (1643-1727)	p.35
1649	King Charles I was executed.	p.33
1649	England declared itself a republic, called the Commonwealth.	p.34
1649	Oliver Cromwell was made leader of the Republic and was given title of 'Lord Protector'.	p.34
1656	The first Jews to come to Britain since the Middle Ages settled in London in 1656.	p.38

Year/ Period	Significant Events	Handbook Page No:
1658	Oliver Cromwell died.	p.34
1649-1658	The only eleven years when England was a republic.	p.34
May 1660	The parliament invited Charles II to come back from exile in the Netherlands.	p.34
1665	Major Outbreak of plague in London	p.35
1666	Great Fire destroyed much of London	p.35
1679	The Habeas Corpus Act became law in 1679.	p.35
1680--1720	Between 1680 and 1720 many refugees called Huguenots came from France.	p.38
1688	The Glorious Revolution by the protestant king of Netherlands, William of Orange, when James II fled to France.	p.36
1689	The Bill of Rights, 1689, confirmed the rights of parliament.	p.37
After 1689	Start of Constitutional Monarchy.	p.38
1690	William defeated James II at the Battle of Boyne in Ireland.	p.36
1695	From 1695, newspapers were allowed to operate without a government licence.	p.38
1707	The Act of union, known as the Treaty of union in Scotland, was agreed.	p.38

Year/ Period	Significant Events	Handbook Page No:
1714	When queen Anne died in 1714, parliament chose a German, George I to be the next King.	p.39
1721	The first man to be called Prime Minister was Sir Robert Walpole, who was prime minister from 1721 to 1742.	p.39
1732	Richard Arkwright (1732 - 92)	p.41
1745	During rule of George II, son of George I, there was another attempt to put a Stuart King back on the throne in place of George I's son, George II	p.39
1746	Battle of Colluden, George II defeated Charles Edward Stuart (Bonnie Prince Charlie).	p.39
1759	Sake Dean Mahomet (1759 - 1851)	p.42
1759	Robert Burns (1759 - 96)	p.40
1760	By the 1760s, there were substantial colonies in North America.	p.43
1776	In 1776, 13 American colonies declared their independence.	p.43
1783	Britain recognised the colonies' independence in 1783.	p.44
1789	French Revolution, waged war on Britain, Napolean continued the war.	p.44

Year/ Period	Significant Events	Handbook Page No:
18th century	The Enlightenment [new ideas.. Politics, industries etc...]	p.40
18th century	Slavery was a fully established overseas industry, dominated by Britain and American colonies.	p.42
Late 1700's	The first formal anti-slavery groups were set up by the Quakers.	p.43
1800	Act of Union of Ireland passed	p.45
1801	In 1801, Ireland became unified with England, Scotland and Wales after the act of Union of 1800.	p.45
1805	Britain's navy fought against combined French and Spanish fleets, winning the Battle of Trafalgar in 1805.	p.44
1807	In 1807, it became illegal to trade slaves in British ships or from British ports.	p.43
1815	In 1815, the French wars ended with the defeat of the emperor Napoleon by the Duke of Wellington at the Battle of Waterloo.	p.44
1832	The Reform Act of 1832 had greatly increased the number of people with the right to vote.	p.50
1833	The Emancipation Act abolished slavery throughout the British Empire.	p.43

Year/ Period	Significant Events	Handbook Page No:
1833	After 1833, 2 million Indian and Chinese workers were employed to replace the freed slaves.	p.43
1837	In 1837, Queen Victoria became queen of the UK at the age of 18.	p.47
1846	Repealing of the Corn Laws	p.47
1847	The number of hours that women and children could work was limited by law to 10 hours per day.	p.47
Victorian Period	A major expansion of the railways took place in the Victorian period.	p.48
1851	A Great Exhibition of machines and handmade goods opened in Hyde Park in the Crystal Palace	p.49
1853-1913	13 million British citizens left the country.	p.47
1853-1856	Britain fought Crimean War, with Turkey and France against Russia.	p.49
1854	In 1854, Florence Nightingale went to turkey and treated soldiers who were fighting in the Crimean war.	p.49
1858	Emmeline Pankhurst was born in Manchester in 1858.	p.51

Year/ Period	Significant Events	Handbook Page No:
1860	In 1860 Florence Nightingale established the Nightingale Training School for nurses at St Thomas' Hospital in London.	p.49
1861	Potato crops failed in mid-19th century, causing famine and emigration. By 1861 there were large populations of Irish people in cities such as Liverpool, London, Manchester and Glasgow.	p.49
1865	Rudyard Kipling was born in India in 1865. [Nobel prize 1907].	p.52
1867	in 1867 there was another Reform Act.	p.50
1870-1914	120,000 Russian and Polish Jews came to Britain to escape persecution.	p.47
1870	Acts of parliament in 1870 and 1882 gave wives the right to keep their own earnings and property.	p.50
1872	The first tennis club was founded in Leamington Spa in 1872.	p.89
1874	Winston Churchill (1874 - 1965)	p.56
1881	Alexander Fleming (1881 - 1955)	p.60
1882	Acts of parliament in 1870 and 1882 gave wives the right to keep their own earnings and property.	p.50

Year/ Period	Significant Events	Handbook Page No:
1889	Emmeline Pankhurst set up The Women's Franchise League in 1889.	p.51
1895	The national trust was founded in 1895 by three volunteers.	p.107
1896	Films were first shown publicly in the UK in 1896.	p.103
1899-1902	The Boer War, when British went to war in South Africa with settlers from Netherlands called the Boers.	p.51
19th century	The Irish nationalist movement had grown strongly.	p.50
19th century	The first professional football clubs were formed in the late 19th century.	p.87
19th-20th century	In the late 19th and early 20th centuries, an increasing number of women [later known as 'suffragettes'] campaigned and demonstrated for greater rights and, in particular, the right to vote.	p.50
20th century	In the 20th century. Sir Edwin Lutyens had an influence throughout the British Empire. He designed New Delhi to be the seat of government in India.	p.96
1901	End of Queen Victoria's reign	p.47
1902	Motor-car racing in the UK started in 1902.	p.89

Year/ Period	Significant Events	Handbook Page No:
1903	In 1903 Emmeline Pankhurst helped found the Women's Social & Political Union (WSPU), the first group whose members were called 'suffragettes'.	p.51
1907	Rudyard Kipling was awarded the Nobel Prize in literature in 1907.	p.52
1908	The UK has hosted the Olympic Games on three occasions: 1908, 1948 and 2012.	p.84
1913	In 1913, the British government promised 'Home Rule' for Ireland.	p.55
1914-1918	The First World War	p.54
1916	During 1st WW, the British attack on the Somme in July 1916, resulted in about 60,000 British casualties on the first day alone.	p.54
1916	Irish nationalists started an uprising (the Easter Rising) against the British in Dublin.	p.55
1918	The First World War ended at 11.00 am on 11th November 1918 with victory for Britain and its allies.	p.55
1920	British Empire continued to grow until 1920s.	p.51
1920's	The television was developed by Scotsman John Logie Baird (1888 - 1946) in the 1920s.	p.65

Year/ Period	Significant Events	Handbook Page No:
1921	In 1921, a peace treaty was signed with Ireland.	p.55
1922	In 1922, Ireland became two countries.	p.55
1922	The BBC started radio broadcasts in 1922.	p.56
1927	The PROMS has been organised by the British Broadcasting Corporation (BBC) since 1927.	p.90
1928	Alexander Fleming discovered Penicillin.	p.60
1928	The women were given the right to vote at the age of 21, the same as men.	p.51
1928	The UK has had a fully democratic voting system since 1928.	p.133
1929	The world entered the 'Great Depression'.	p.55
1930-1939	Car ownership doubled from 1 million to 2 million.	p.56
1930's	A Turing Machine is a theoretical mathematical device invented by Alan Turing, a British.	p.65
1930's	The Jet Engine was developed in Britain in the 1930s by Sir Frank Whittle, a British Royal air force engineer officer.	p.65
1830's-- 1840's	In the 1830s and 1840s, a group called the Chartists campaigned for reform.	p.120

Year/ Period	Significant Events	Handbook Page No:
1932	Scotsman John Logie Baird made the first television broadcast between London and Glasgow.	p.65
1933	Adolf Hitler came to power in Germany in 1933.	p.56
1935	Radar was developed by Scotsman Sir Robert Watson-Watt (1892 – 1973).	p.65
1935	Movie: The 39 Steps (1935), directed by Alfred Hitchcock.	p.104
1936	The BBC started the world's first regular television service in 1936.	p.56
1939	Hitler invaded Poland in 1939.	p.56
1940	Winston Churchill became prime minister.	p.56
1940	German forces defeated allied troops and advanced through France.	p.56
1941	Japanese bombed America's naval base at Pearl Harbour.	p.58
1941	America joined 2nd WW when above happened.	p.58
1942	Beveridge Report presented by William Beveridge [the 1942 report Social Insurance and Allied Services].	p.62

Year/ Period	Significant Events	Handbook Page No:
1944	6 June 1944, [2nd WW] allied forces landed in Normandy (this event is often referred to as 'D-Day').	p.59
1944	The introduction of Education Act 1944 (often called 'The Butler act'), by conservative MP, RA Butler.	p.62
1945	The allies comprehensively defeated Germany in May 1945.	p.59
1945	The war against Japan ended in august 1945 when the United States dropped its newly developed atom bombs on the Japanese cities of Hiroshima and Nagasaki.	p.59
1945	Winston Churchill lost the general election in 1945.	p.56
1945	Labour government elected in Britain	p.60
1945	Clement Attlee became prime minister after the labour party won the 1945 election.	p.61
1947	In 1947, independence was granted to nine countries including India, Pakistan, Ceylon (now Sri Lanka).	p.61
1948	NHS established under Labour government.	p.60
1948	Benefits were introduced.	p.60
1948	In 1948, people from West Indies were invited to come and work.	p.63

Year/ Period	Significant Events	Handbook Page No:
1948	The UK has hosted the Olympic Games on three occasions: 1908, 1948 and 2012.	p.84
20th century	By the second half of the 20th century, Britain gave freedom to commonwealth countries.	p.52
1949	The independent part of Ireland became Irish Republic.	p.55
1950	UK signed European Convention on Human Rights and Fundamental Freedoms	p.148
1950's	The 1950s were a period of economic recovery after the war.	p.61
1950's	Sir Christopher Cockerell (1910 -99), a British inventor, invented hovercraft in the 1950s	p.65
1950's	There was a shortage of labour in the UK.	p.63
1951-1964	Conservative government	p.61
1951	Churchill returned as PM.	p.56
1952	Queen Elizabeth II has been reigning since her father's death in 1952.	p.122
1952	The Mousetrap, a murder-mystery play by Dame Agatha Christie, has been running in the West End since 1952and has had the longest initial run of any show in history.	p.93

Year/ Period	Significant Events	Handbook Page No:
1954	Sir Roger Bannister was the first man in world to run a mile in under four minutes, in 1954.	p.85
1957	West Germany, France, Belgium, Italy, Luxembourg and the Netherlands formed the European Economic Community (EEC)	p.66
1958	Since 1958, the prime minister has had the power to nominate peers just for their own lifetime.	p.124
1950's--60's	The 1950s and 1960s were a high point for British comedies, including Passport to Pimlico, The Ladykillers and, later, the Carry On films.	p.103
1960's	Swinging sixties' known for growth in British fashion, cinema and popular music.	p.63
1960's	The 1960s was also a time of technological progress.	p.63
1960's	In late 1960s because the government passed new laws to restrict immigration to Britain.	p.64
1962	Lawrence of Arabia (1962), directed by David Lean.	p.104
1964	Churchill stood down as an MP.	p.56
1965	Winston Churchill died.	p.56

Year/ Period	Significant Events	Handbook Page No:
1966	England's only Football international Tournament victory was at the world cup of 1966 hosted in the UK.	p.88
1966-67	A British sailor, Sir Francis Chichester, was the first person to sail single-handed around the world, in 1966/67.	p.89
1967	The first ATM machine [invented by James Goodfellow] was put into use by Barclays Bank in Enfield, north London in 1967.	p.65
1969	Troubles broke out in Northern Ireland.	p.131
1969	Present voting age of 18 was set.	p.132
1969	Britain and France developed Concorde, the world's only supersonic passenger aircraft. First flew in 1969; began carrying passengers in 1976; Retired from service in 2003.	p.65
1970's	Britain admitted 28,000 people of Indian origin who had been forced to leave Uganda.	p.64
1970's	The 1970s were also a time of serious unrest in Northern Ireland.	p.66
1972	In 1972, the Northern Ireland parliament was suspended.	p.66
1972	Mary Peters who won an Olympic gold medal in the pentathlon in 1972.	p.66
1973	UK joined European Union [previously EEC]	p.66

Year/ Period	Significant Events	Handbook Page No:
1978	IVF (In-vitro fertilisation) therapy for the treatment of infertility was pioneered in Britain. The world's first 'test tube baby' was born in Oldham, Lancashire in 1978.	p.65
1979-1990	Margaret Thatcher, Britain's first woman prime minister, led the Conservative government from 1979 to 1990.	p.66
1979-1990	There was privatisation of nationalised industries and imposed legal controls on trade union powers.	p.67
1982	Argentina invaded the Falkland Islands.	p.67
1984	The Turner Prize was established in 1984 and celebrates contemporary art.	p.95
1990	World wide web was invented by Sir Tim Berners-Lee, a British.	p.65
1990's	Throughout the 1990s, Britain played a leading role in coalition forces involved in the liberation of Kuwait, following the Iraqi invasion in 1990.	p.68
1990's	Britain involved in the conflict in the Former Republic of Yugoslavia.	p.68
1996	Two British scientists, Sir Ian Wilmot and Keith Campbell were the first to succeed in cloning a mammal, Dolly the sheep.	p.65
1997-2010	Labour government elected	p.68

Year/ Period	Significant Events	Handbook Page No:
1997-2010	Labour government elected	p.68
1997	In 1997 the Labour party led by Tony Blair was elected.	p.68
1998	In Northern Ireland, the Belfast Agreement or the Good Friday Agreement was signed in 1998.	p.68
1998	The Human Rights Act 1998 incorporated in the European Convention on Human Rights into UK law.	p.149
1999	Since 1999, hereditary peers have lost the automatic right to attend the House of Lords.	p.124
1999	Scottish parliament and a Welsh Assembly were introduced	p.68
1999	The Northern Ireland assembly was elected in 1999.	p.68
2000	Since 2000, British armed forces have been engaged in the global fight against international terrorism... , including operations in Afghanistan and Iraq.	p.68
2002	The Northern Ireland assembly was suspended in 2002.	p.68
2002	Winston Churchill was voted the greatest Briton of all time by the public.	p.56

Year/ Period	Significant Events	Handbook Page No:
2003	In 2003, The Lord of the Rings by JRR Tolkien was voted the country's best- loved novel.	p.97
2004	Dame Kelly Holmes won two gold medals for running in the 2004 Olympic Games.	p.85
2004	Dame Ellen MacArthur, a yachtswoman became the fastest person to sail around the world singlehanded	p.85
2007	The Northern Ireland assembly reinstated.	p.68
2007	Gordon brown took over as prime minister in 2007.	p.68
2007	Forced Marriage (Civil Protection) Act 2007, was introduced.	p.150
2008	Forced Marriage Protection Orders were introduced in 2008 for England, Wales and Northern Ireland	p.150
2009	British combat troops left Iraq in 2009.	p.68
2010	Census, showing UK population of just over 62 Million	p.74
2012	Queen's Diamond Jubilee was celebrated.	p.122
2012	The UK has hosted the Olympic Games on three occasions: 1908, 1948 and 2012.	p.84

Year/ Period	Significant Events	Handbook Page No:
2012	Mo Farah won gold medals in the 2012 Olympics for the 5000 and 10,000 metres and is the first Briton to win the Olympic Gold medal in the 10,000 metres.	p.86
2012	Jessica Ennis won the 2012 Olympic gold medal in the heptathlon.	p.86
2012	Scottish tennis player, Andy Murray won the men's singles in the US Open.	p.86
2012	Bradley Wiggins, a cyclist, became the first Briton to win the Tour de France.	p.86
2012	The Big Ben clock tower named 'Elizabeth Tower' in honour of Queen Elizabeth II's Diamond Jubilee in 2012.	p.108
2012	In November 2012, the public elected police and crime commissioners (PCCS) in England and Wales.	p.142
2014	Afghans will have full security responsibility in all provinces by the end of 2014.	p.69

Section 2

Chapter wise Practice Questions

Chapter 1:

The Values & Principles of the UK

Chapter 2:

What is The UK?

1   **Which of the following statements is correct?**

    A   Britain welcomes new residents because they add diversity to national life

    B   Britain welcomes new residents because they bring huge sums of money for British people

****

2   **British society is founded on which of these?**

    A   Wealth

    B   Religion

    C   Fundamental values and principles

    D   Science

****

3   **Who should support fundamental values and principles?**

    A   Only immigrants

    B   All those living in UK

    C   Politicians

    D   Students

****

4   **British values are based on which TWO of these?**

    A   Scientific facts only

    B   History

    C   Traditions

    D   Law only

****

5   **Who is allowed to show intolerance and extremism in UK?**

    A   Only Police

    B   Only government departments

    C   Only judges

    D   No one

****

6   Which TWO of these are the fundamental principles of British life?

      A   Democracy & Individual liberty
      B   Growing your own vegetable
      C   Tolerance of different faiths and beliefs
      D   Recycling

****

7   At what time do the new citizens pledge to uphold British values?

      A   When they apply for test
      B   When they apply for permanent residence
      C   At Citizenship Ceremony
      D   Anytime in life

****

8   Which TWO of these should you do if you wish to be a permanent resident or citizen of the UK?

      A   Respect and Obey Law
      B   Respect others' rights and opinions
      C   Pay extra taxes
      D   Join Army

****

9   Which TWO does UK offer to its citizens?

      A   Freedom of speech
      B   Freedom of belief and religion
      C   Free US Visas
      D   Free Housing for all immigrants

****

10   Which TWO do you need in order to apply for permanent residency or citizenship of the UK?

A   Have good understanding of life in the UK

B   Can speak and read English

C   £50,000 in your bank

D   Own car and home

****

11   The Life in the UK Test questions require an understanding of the English language at what level?

A   ESOL entry level 1
B   ESOL entry level 2
C   ESOL entry level 3
D   ESOL entry level 4

****

12   People on work visas are not required to pass 'Life in the UK test' to become permanent residents. Is this statement true or false?

A   True
B   False

****

13   If your standard of English is below ESOL Entry level 3, which of these will you need before you can apply for your permanent residence?

A   Life in the UK Test and an English language Test

B   Only an English Language Test

C   Pass an ESOL Course in English with Citizenship, with a test in the end

D   Only Life in the UK test

****

14   Once you pass Life in the UK test, you can make an application for permanent residence free of charge. Is this statement true or false?

        A   True
        B   False

****

15   The forms to make an application for permanent residence can be found at which of these websites?

        A   Home office's UKBA website.
        B   HMRC Website
        C   Life in the UK Test Website
        D   Local Council Website

****

16   Currently [April 2013], if you pass Life in the UK test, you do not need to appear in a separate English test. Is this statement true or false?
        A   True
        B   False

****

17   From October 2013, evidence of English language skills at B1 level of European framework will be compulsory to apply for citizenship. Is this true or false?

        A   True
        B   False

** *******

18   The requirements for British Citizenship may change in future. Where should you check for information before applying for citizenship?

        A   DVLA Website
        B   HMRC Website
        C   Life in the UK Test Website
        D   Home office's UKBA website.

****

19   Life in the UK test can be given in which TWO of these language/s in addition to English?

  A   Welsh
  B   Scottish Gaelic
  C   Spanish
  D   French

****

20   You can appear in Life in the UK test at which of these places?

  A   Any local library
  B   Your own school or University
  C   Online at UKBA website
  D   Only approved and Registered Life in the UK Test centres

****

21   There are different arrangements for taking the life in the UK test in the Isle of Man or in the Channel Islands. Is this statement true or false?

  A   True
  B   False

****

22   Which of the following do you need to take to the test?

  A   Current valid visa & proof of ID
  B   Proof of address & ID
  C   Proof of ID & application fee
  D   Proof of English language skills

****

23   If you forget to take with you all the required documents to the test, the test centre staff will do which of these?

      A   Allow you to sit the test with a warning

      B   Allow you to go back home and bring documents and will wait for you before starting the test

      C   Will return your fee and ask you to re-apply when you have documents

      D   Will not allow you to sit the test and your fee will be forfeited

****

24   The UK border agency website, provides information about the Citizenship application process. Is this statement true or false?

      A   True
      B   False

****

25   The life in the UK test website provides information about the test and how to book a place to take one. Is this statement true or false?

      A   True
      B   False

****

26   The website Gov.uk provides information about ESOL courses and how to find one in your area. Is this statement true or false?

      A   True
      B   False

****

27   What is the official name of Great Britain?

    A   Britain

    B   United Kingdom of Great Britain

    C   United Kingdom of Great Britain and Northern Ireland

    D   Great Britain

****

28   What does Great Britain refer to?

    A   England and Scotland

    B   England, Scotland and Wales

    C   England, Scotland and Northern Ireland

    D   England and Wales

****

29   What is the UK made up of?

    A   England and Scotland

    B   England, Scotland and Wales

    C   England, Scotland, Wales and Northern Ireland

    D   England and Wales

****

30   Which of these are Crown Dependencies or territories?

    A   Channel Islands & Isle of Man

    B   Ireland and Isle of Wight

    C   Australia

    D   Canada

****

31   Which of these are British overseas territories?

        A   Germany
        B   Australia
        C   Falkland Islands
        D   Dunkirk

****

32   Where does the UK parliament sit?

        A   Kings Cross in London
        B   Westminster
        C   Cambridge
        D   Oxford

****

33   Scotland, Wales and Northern Ireland also have parliaments or assemblies of their own. Is this statement true or false?

        A   True
        B   False

****

ANSWER KEY

Q.#	Answer	Reference	
		Chapter	Page No.
1.	A	The Values & Principles of the UK	p. 7
2.	C	The Values & Principles of the UK	p. 7
3.	B	The Values & Principles of the UK	p. 7
4.	B & C	The Values & Principles of the UK	p. 7
5.	D	The Values & Principles of the UK	p. 7
6.	A & C	The Values & Principles of the UK	p. 7-8
7.	C	The Values & Principles of the UK	p. 8
8.	A & B	The Values & Principles of the UK	p. 8
9.	A & B	The Values & Principles of the UK	p. 8
10.	C	The Values & Principles of the UK	p. 8 - 9
11.	B	The Values & Principles of the UK	p. 9
12.	B	The Values & Principles of the UK	p. 9
13.	C	The Values & Principles of the UK	p. 9
14.	B	The Values & Principles of the UK	p. 9
15.	A	The Values & Principles of the UK	p. 9
16.	A	The Values & Principles of the UK	p. 9
17.	A	The Values & Principles of the UK	p. 9
18.	D	The Values & Principles of the UK	p. 9
19.	A & B	The Values & Principles of the UK	p. 10
20.	D	The Values & Principles of the UK	p. 10
21.	A	The Values & Principles of the UK	p. 10
22.	B	The Values & Principles of the UK	p. 10

ANSWER KEY

Q.#	Answer	Reference	
		Chapter	Page No.
23.	D	The Values & Principles of the UK	p. 10
24.	A	The Values & Principles of the UK	p. 11
25.	A	The Values & Principles of the UK	p. 11
26.	A	The Values & Principles of the UK	p. 11
27.	C	What is the UK?	p. 13
28.	B	What is the UK?	p. 13
29.	C	What is the UK?	p. 13
30.	A	What is the UK?	p. 13
31.	C	What is the UK?	p. 13
32.	B	What is the UK?	p. 13
33.	A	What is the UK?	p. 13

Chapter 3:

A Long & Illustrious History

1   What were the first people to live in Britain?

      A   Merchants
      B   Farmers
      C   Industrialists
      D   Hunter-gatherers

****

2   In Stone age, the first ever people to come to Britain, found their way following which of these?

      A   Brave Kings & Emperors
      B   A trail of treasure
      C   Herds of deers and horses which they hunted
      D   Stars

****

3   In the Stone Age, Britain was connected to the continent by which of these?

      A   Culture & Traditions
      B   Religion
      C   Land Bridge
      D   Tunnels

****

4   Britain became permanently separated from the Continent, by the Channel, how long ago?

      A   100 years ago
      B   1000 years ago
      C   10,000 years ago
      D   Million years ago

****

5   **When did the first farmers arrive in Britain?**

     A   After Jesus Christ

     B   After second world war

     C   Million years ago

     D   6000 years ago

6   **Where did the ancestors of the first ever farmers in Britain come from?**

     A   Scotland

     B   Ireland

     C   Europe

     D   Asia

7   **What is Stonehenge?**

     A   A process of cutting big stones

     B   A famous British actor

     C   An old monument in Wiltshire

     D   A cook book

8   **Stonehenge was probably a place for which of these?**

     A   Ceremonies

     B   Laundry

     C   Stoning witches

     D   Farming

9   Best preserved prehistoric village in Northern Europe is in Scotland. What is its name?

        A   Inverness
        B   Edinburgh
        C   Skara Brae
        D   Skatic village

****

10   Bronze Age is called 'bronze' because of which of these reasons?

        A   Men discovered bronze mountains
        B   Most of the animals had a bronze look
        C   It was an age when Sun went bronze
        D   People learned to make bronze

****

11   Which period was called Stone Age?

        A   1000 years ago
        B   6000 years ago
        C   10,000 years ago
        D   Million years ago

****

12   Which period was called Bronze Age?

        A   1000 years ago
        B   6000 years ago
        C   10,000 years ago
        D   Million years ago

****

13   Prehistoric people used to live in which of these?

     A   Round houses
     B   Round Burrows
     C   Square houses
     D   Tomb Burrows

14   Prehistoric people used to bury their deads in which of these?

     A   Round houses
     B   Round Burrows
     C   Square houses
     D   Tomb Burrows

15   People of Bronze Age were expert in which field?

     A   Medicine
     B   Farming
     C   Metalwork
     D   Swimming

16   In Iron Age, people sometimes defended sites called which of these?

     A   Round houses
     B   Bronze houses
     C   Stone Houses
     D   Hill Forts

17   A very impressive hill fort can still be seen today at which of these?

    A   Maiden Castle, Dorset
    B   Edinburgh, Scotland
    C   Glasgow
    D   Lake District, England

****

18   The language they spoke in Iron Age was a part of which language?

    A   French
    B   Latin
    C   Celtic
    D   Welsh

****

19   The people of Iron Age had a sophisticated culture and economy. Is this statement true or false?

    A   True
    B   False

****

20   The first coins were minted in Britain in as early as which of these?

    A   Stone Age
    B   Bronze Age
    C   Iron Age
    D   Middle Age

*** ************

21   When did the Romans first come to Britain with Julius Caesar?

    A   55 BC
    B   65 BC
    C   82 BC
    D   91 BC

****

22   The first Roman invasion in 55BC was successful in conquering Britain. Is this statement true or false?

    A   True
    B   False

****

23   Who led the second Roman invasion to Britain in AD 43?

    A   Alexander the Great
    B   Julius Caesar
    C   Emperor Claudius
    D   Hitler

****

24   Who was Boudicca? Mark TWO answers.

    A   The Queen of Iceni
    B   A tribal leader who fought against Romans
    C   A Stone Age tradition
    D   A bronze monument

****

25   Where is the statue of Boudicca?

    A   Edinburgh
    B   Oxford
    C   Westminster Bridge, London
    D   Cambridge

26   **What area of Britain was never conquered by Romans?**

    A   Scotland
    B   Cornwall
    C   Wales
    D   London

27   **Who built a wall in the north of England to keep out the Picts (ancestors of the Scottish people)?**

    A   Alexander the Great
    B   Julius Caesar
    C   Emperor Claudius
    D   Emperor Hadrian

28   **For how long did the Romans remain in Britain?**

    A   2000 years
    B   200 years
    C   4000 years
    D   400 years

29   **What did Romans do in Britain?**

    A   Built Roads
    B   Killed people
    C   Ruined the area
    D   Made Laws

30   When did first Christians came to Britain?

       A   1000 years after Christ
       B   3rd & 4th centuries AD
       C   55 BC
       D   43 AD

****

31   When did Romans leave Britain?

       A   210 AD
       B   410 AD
       C   1000 AD
       D   2000 AD

****

32   Why did Romans leave Britain?

       A   They did not like British weather
       B   They had angered locals
       C   To defend other parts of the Roman Empire
       D   To attack France

****

33   Which tribes invaded Britain after Romans? Mark TWO correct answers.

       A   Jutes
       B   Arabs
       C   Angles & Saxons
       D   Americans

****

34   When were the Anglo-Saxon kingdoms established in Britain?

  A 210 AD

  B 410 AD

  C 600 AD

  D 55 BC

35   Which king was buried with his treasure in Suffolk?

  A William of Orange

  B King James I

  C Emperor Claudius

  D Sutton Hoo

36   When Anglo Saxons first came to Britain, which of these is true about their religion?

  A They were not Christians

  B They were Catholic Christians

  C They were Protestant Christians

  D They were Orthodox Christians

37   Who was the patron saint of Ireland?

  A St Patrick

  B St Columba

  C St Augustine

  D St George

38   Which of these became the first Archbishop of Canterbury?

    A   St Patrick

    B   St Columbia

    C   St Augustine

    D   St George

****

39   Where did St Columbia found his monastery?

    A   Columbia

    B   Scotland

    C   England

    D   Ireland

****

40   Where did Vikings come from? Mark TWO answers.

    A   France

    B   Denmark

    C   Italy

    D   Norway

****

41   When did Vikings first visit Britain?

    A   55 BC

    B   43 AD

    C   AD 789

    D   1914

****

42   **Why did Vikings first visit Britain?**

       A   To conquer Britain

       B   To establish trade

       C   To raid towns & take away slaves and goods

       D   To meet the king

43   **Where did Vikings make their communities?**

       A   Wales

       B   East of England

       C   Scotland

       D   Ireland

44   **Who defeated the Vikings?**

       A   King Alfred

       B   Sir Winston Churchill

       C   Julius Caesar

       D   Hitler

45   **Danish kings ruled England for a short period. Which of these was the first Danish king in England?**

       A   King Cnut or Canute

       B   Julius Caesar

       C   Emperor Claudius

       D   Emperor Hadrian

46   **Kenneth MacAlpin was a Welsh king. Is this statement true or false?**

       A   True

       B   False

47 William the conqueror came from which country to conquer Britain?

    A   Rome

    B   Scotland

    C   Ireland

    D   France

48 Bayeux Tapestry is a piece of embroidery, made in memory of which of these?

    A   Roman invasion

    B   Battle of Hastings

    C   Battle of Waterloo

    D   Battle of Bannockburn

49 William the conqueror fought which battle to conquer Britain?

    A   Battle of Hastings

    B   Battle of Waterloo

    C   War of Roses

    D   Battle of Bannockburn

50 In which year did 'William the Conqueror' conquer England?

    A   1943

    B   410

    C   1066

    D   900

51   The Norman conquest was the last successful foreign invasion of England. Is this statement true or false?

   A   True
   B   False

****

52   Which of the following statements is correct?

   A   Normans invaded and conquered Scotland
   B   Normans took over some land on the border but did not invade Scotland

****

53   What did the Domesday book [formed after Norman conquest] contain? Mark TWO answers.

   A   List of people in towns and villages
   B   List of lands owned by people
   C   Knowledge of Christianity
   D   Knowledge of Astrology

****

54   What is the period from Norman conquest to 1485 called?

   A   Iron Age
   B   Bronze Age
   C   Middle Ages
   D   War Age

****

55   In 1284, the Statute of Rhuddlan annexed which country to England?

   A   Wales
   B   Scotland
   C   Ireland
   D   Channel Islands

****

56   When did English defeat Welsh rebellions and introduce
           English laws and language?

           A   12th century
           B   19th century
           C   15th century
           D   20th century

****

57   In which battle did Scottish, led by Robert the Bruce,
           defeat English?

           A   Battle of Hastings
           B   Battle of Waterloo
           C   Battle of Bannockburn
           D   Battle of Roses

****

58   When did Scottish, led by Robert the Bruce, defeat
           English?

           A   1284
           B   1314
           C   1450
           D   1200

****

59   When was Scotland conquered by English?

           A   1285
           B   1914
           C   1889
           D   Never

****

60   In which year did Scots join England in an Act of Union?

       A   1828

       B   1707

       C   1642

       D   1727

****

61   Why did English troops first go to Ireland?

       A   To kill the Irish king

       B   To help the Irish king

       C   To trade

       D   For Fishing

****

62   By 1200, the English ruled an area of Ireland around Dublin, known as which of these?

       A   Pale

       B   Isle of Wight

       C   Rush

       D   Bray

****

63   What were the wars the European Christians fought for control of Holy land called?

       A   World Wars

       B   Holy Wars

       C   Crusades

       D   Cascades

****

64   When did the English kings fight wars for control of Holy land?

     A   Middle Ages
     B   Iron Age
     C   Early 20th century
     D   Just before First World War

65   What was the battle in which English defeat French at the end of 100 year war?

     A   Battle of Hastings
     B   Battle of Agincourt
     C   Battle of Waterloo
     D   Battle of Bannockburn

66   Which English King defeated French at the end of the Hundred Years' War in 1415?

     A   King Charles I
     B   King Edward I
     C   King James II
     D   King Henry V

67   What was the system of land ownership that Normans introduced?

     A   Council Land
     B   War land
     C   Feudalism
     D   Centralism

68   Normans introduced a system in which land was given in exchange for which of these?

    A   Gold Schillings
    B   Help in farming
    C   Help in War
    D   Help in Education

69   In the north of Scotland and Ireland, land was owned by members of 'clans' (prominent families). Is this statement true or false?

    A   True
    B   False

70   In which year was there Black Death in England?

    A   1428
    B   1524
    C   1345
    D   1348

71   Which areas of Britain were affected by Black death?

    A   England, Scotland & Wales
    B   England & Wales Only
    C   England & Scotland
    D   Scotland & Wales

72   After Black death, which of these happened?

    A   Peasants were ready to work at very low wages
    B   Peasants began to demand higher wages

73   When people left countryside and moved to towns, a new
        social class developed, which was?

        A   Upper Class
        B   Aristocracy
        C   Middle Class
        D   Lower Class

74   In Ireland also, the Black Death killed many in the Pale. Is
        this statement true or false?

        A   True
        B   False

75   Did the kings have more or less powers until 1215?

        A   More
        B   Less

76   Which king was forced to sign Magna Carta or the Greater
        Charter?

        A   William the Conqueror
        B   King Edward I
        C   King James II
        D   King John

77   What did Magna Carta establish?

        A   That king was a Godly Figure
        B   That even the king was subject to law
        C   That slavery should be abolished
        D   That poor have equal rights

****

78 **In the Middle Ages, who sat in House of Lords? Mark TWO answers.**

A   Nobility

B   Soldiers

C   Bishops

D   Traders

****

79 **In the Middle Ages, who sat in House of Commons? Mark TWO answers.**

A   Smaller land owners

B   Poor people

C   Monarch

D   Wealthy people from towns and cities

****

80 **Scottish Parliament had three 'Houses' called 'Estates' during the Middle Ages. Which of these is NOT one of the three Estates?**

A   Lords

B   Saints

C   Clergy

D   Commons

****

81 **How did the judges develop common law in England?**

A   Judges asked the kings

B   Pope dictated the laws

C   Laws were based on precedence and tradition.

D   Laws were imported from neighbouring countries

****

82   In Scotland, the laws are codified or written down. Is this
        statement true or false?

        A   True
        B   False

****

83   After Norman Conquest Anglo-Saxon and French
        languages combined to form English . Is this statement
        true or false?

        A   True
        B   False

****

84   In English language, which TWO of these words came
        from French?

        A   Beauty
        B   Summer
        C   Ask
        D   Demand

****

85   In which year did English become the preferred language
        of Royal Court?

        A   300 BC
        B   1400
        C   1800
        D   2001

****

86   In years leading to 1400, Geoffrey Chaucer wrote a series of poems in English. What were these called?

    A   The Chaucer Poems

    B   The Royal Poems

    C   The Canterbury Tales

    D   The Chaucer's Tales

****

87   Who was the first person in England to print books using a printing press?

    A   Robinhood

    B   Florence Nightingale

    C   Neil Armstrong

    D   William Caxton

****

88   Who wrote 'The Bruce' about the Battle of Bannockburn?

    A   Robert Wallace

    B   John Barbour

    C   Bruce Willis

    D   Scottish Government

****

89   Which TWO of the following castles from Middle Ages, are still in use?

    A   Windsor Castle

    B   Edinburgh Castle

    C   Nottingham Castle

    D   Conwy Castle

****

90   In Middle Ages, several cathedrals were built which had windows of stained glass, telling stories about which of these?

      A   Stone Age Man

      B   War times

      C   Bible & Christian Saints

      D   Moses & Pharaoh

****

91   Regarding Britain in Middle ages, which TWO of these are true?

      A   Britain was ruined by drugs

      B   Americans ruled Britain

      C   England was an important trading nation

      D   English wool became a very important export

****

92   In middle ages, which of these skilled people come to Britain? Mark TWO answers.

      A   Glass manufacturers from Italy

      B   Weavers from France

      C   Engineers from America

      D   Warriors from Australia

****

93   In 1455, War of Roses was fought to decide which of these?

      A   Which should be the official church of England

      B   Who should be king of England

****

94   In 1455, War of Roses was fought between which two groups?

    A   House of Lords & House of Commons

    B   House of Elizabeth & House of Henry

    C   House of Lancaster & House of York

    D   England and Wales

****

95   War of Roses was called War of the Roses, because the symbol of Lancaster was a red rose and the symbol of York was a white rose. Is this statement true or false?

    A   True

    B   False

****

96   Who won the War of Roses?

    A   Hitler

    B   King Edward I

    C   King James II

    D   King Henry VII

****

97   War of Roses began in 1455 and ended in 1485, with which of these battles?

    A   Battle of Hastings

    B   Battle of Bosworth

    C   Battle of Waterloo

    D   Battle of Bannockburn

****

98   Whom did Henry VII [Henry Tudor] marry after War of Roses?

    A   Elizabeth of York

    B   Queen Victoria

    C   Florence Nightingale

    D   Mary Poppins

****

99   What was the symbol of the house of Tudor?

    A   A white rose

    B   A red rose

    C   A red rose with a white rose inside it

    D   Two white roses

****

100   Who established the Church of England?

    A   William the Conqueror

    B   Tom Cruise

    C   Henry VIII

    D   King James

****

101   The Church of England was established because the Pope refused to allow Henry VIII to divorce his wife. Is this statement true or false?

    A   True

    B   False

****

102   In Church of England, who has the power to appoint bishops?

    A   Monarch

    B   Pope

    C   Prime Minister

    D   Public

****

103   Reformation was a movement against which of these?

    A   The authority of King

    B   The authority of Pope

    C   The Hitler

    D   All of these

****

104   Who were the Protestants?

    A   People always involved in protests

    B   People who opposed the king

    C   People who opposed the Pope

    D   People who favoured the Pope

****

105   Which of these is true about protestants?

    A   They formed their own Churches, read bible in their own languages instead of in Latin; they did not pray to saints or at shrines

    B   They formed their own Churches, read bible in Latin; they prayed a lot to saints or at shrines

****

106   Protestants believed in each person's own relationship with God. Is this statement true or false?

    A   True

    B   False

107   Attempts by English to impose their protestant ideas led to rebellion and brutal fighting in which country?

  A   Scotland
  B   Wales
  C   Ireland
  D   France

108   Wales became formally united with England by which of these?

  A   Magna Carta
  B   Act for the Government of Wales
  C   Euro Tunnel
  D   Welsh Assembly

109   Which book was written during the reign of Edward VI, to be used in Church of England?

  A   Edward VI's Bible
  B   Hansard
  C   Domesday Book
  D   The Book of Common Prayer

110   Henry VIII's daughter Queen Mary, was a devout catholic and persecuted protestants and was called which of these?

  A   Catholic Mary
  B   Virgin Mary
  C   Bloody Mary
  D   Rosy Mary

****

111   After Queen Mary, who re-established the Church of England as official Church in England?

A   Queen Elizabeth I
B   Queen Victoria
C   Queen Elizabeth II
D   Charles I

****

112   Queen Elizabeth I was the half sister of 'Bloody Mary'. Is this statement true or false?

A   True
B   False

****

113   Which of the following statements is correct?

A   Elizabeth I became one of the most disliked monarchs in English history
B   Elizabeth I became one of the most popular monarchs in English history

****

114   In 1588, under Elizabeth I's rule, English got defeated by Spanish armada. Is this statement true or false?

A   True
B   False

****

115   In 1560, Roman Catholic Church services became illegal in which country?

     A   Scotland
     B   England
     C   Ireland
     D   Wales

116   Mary, the queen of Scots was a cousin of Elizabeth I. Is this statement true or false?

     A   False
     B   True

117   Where was Mary, the queen of Scots executed?

     A   Edinburgh
     B   Glasgow
     C   England
     D   France

118   Which of the following statements is correct?

     A   Mary the queen of Scots was executed because she killed Elizabeth I's husband.

     B   Mary the queen of Scots was executed because Elizabeth I suspected she wanted to take over her throne

119   Elizabethan period is known for which of these? Mark TWO answers.

    A   Patriotism

    B   World War 1

    C   New Trade Routes

    D   Inventions

****

120   Who was the founder of England's naval tradition?

    A   Winston Churchill

    B   Margaret Thatcher

    C   Sir Francis Drake

    D   Graham Bell

****

121   What particularly made the English settlers to colonise America?

    A   Trade interests

    B   Weather

    C   Religious disagreements in home country

    D   They went to occupy America

****

122   Which of these is true about Elizabeth I?

    A   King James VI of Scotland was her son and heir

    B   Elizabeth I never married and so had no children of her own to inherit her throne

****

123 Which TWO of these kings established English authority over the whole of the Ireland?

    A   William of Orange
    B   Henry VII
    C   Henry VIII
    D   Charles I

****

124 Who succeeded Elizabeth I?

    A   Queen Mary, also called 'Bloody Mary'
    B   King Edward I
    C   King James II
    D   King James I

****

125 During the reigns of Elizabeth I and James I, lands were taken from Catholics in Ireland and given to English and Scottish Protestants. What were these settlements called?

    A   Plantations
    B   Replacement
    C   Deportations
    D   Emigrations

****

126 Which of these was very skilled at managing parliament?

    A   Elizabeth I
    B   King James I & King Charles I

****

127   Who was the last king who entered the House of Commons, (and tried to arrest five parliamentary leaders)?

     A   William the Conqueror

     B   Charles I

     C   William Shakespeare

     D   Tony Blair

****

128   Which king faced Civil war with his parliament and was finally executed?

     A   William the Conqueror

     B   William of Orange

     C   King Charles I

     D   King Charles II

****

129   What were the people who supported the parliament as opposed to king Charles I, called?

     A   Reporters

     B   Rebellions

     C   Cavaliers

     D   Roundheads

****

130   When did England become a Republic?

     A   1649, after death of Charles I

     B   After first world war

     C   After second World War

     D   After war of roses

****

131   When England became a Republic called Commonwealth, who was recognised as the leader of the new republic?

      A   Adolf Hitler

      B   Winston Churchill

      C   Oliver Cromwell

      D   Tony Blair

132   Which king escaped and fled to Europe, famously hiding on an oak tree on one occasion?

      A   King Alfred

      B   King Edward I

      C   King James II

      D   King Charles II

133   Who was given the title of Lord Protector?

      A   Lord Mountbatten

      B   Winston Churchill

      C   Oliver Cromwell

      D   Tony Blair

134   How long did Britain remain a republic?

      A   100 years

      B   5 years

      C   55 years

      D   11 years

135   Who was invited as king after death of Oliver Cromwell?

    A   Charles II from his escape in Netherlands

    B   William, the Duke of Normandy

    C   King James II

    D   Elizabeth II

136   Which of these happened in reign of Charles II? Mark TWO answers.

    A   Restoration of monarchy

    B   Major Outbreak of Plague

    C   England followed Catholic Church

    D   Pope visited often

137   The Habeas Corpus Act became law in 1679. Why was it made?

    A   It was made so that everybody gets a right to a court hearing and no one could be held prisoner unlawfully

    B   To oppose big corporations

    C   To legalise slave trade

    D   To end Monarchy

138   Which of these kings was interested in science?

    A   King Charles I

    B   King Edward I

    C   King James II

    D   King Charles II

139   **Royal Society was formed to promote which knowledge?**

   A   Religious
   B   Natural
   C   Archaeology
   D   Daily news

****

140   **Sir Edmund Halley successfully predicted the return of the comet, now called which of these?**

   A   Edmund's Comet
   B   Return of the Comet
   C   Halley's Comet
   D   Periodic Comet

****

141   **Why did people in England not want King James II to rule them?**

   A   James II was a Roman Catholic & people in England worried that James wanted to make England a catholic country once more
   B   People in England worried that James will unite with Scotland and crush them

****

142   **William of Orange from Netherlands, invaded England in 1688. What was the invasion called?**

   A   100 years war
   B   War of Roses
   C   War of thorns
   D   The Glorious Revolution

****

143   **Why did some Scots distrusted the new government by King William III (of Orange)?**

     A   Because of the memory of massacre of families which were late in taking the oath.

     B   Because William was a Roman Catholic

****

144   **What were the supporters of the Catholic King James II called?**

     A   Jamnites

     B   Jacobites

     C   Protestants

     D   Puritans

****

145   **What was the Bill of Rights, 1689?**

     A   Bill of rights confirmed power of religion

     B   Bill of Rights confirmed the rights and powers of king

     C   Bill of right confirmed rights of the parliament

     D   Bill of right confirmed rights of immigrants in Britain

****

146   **On which Royal coronation was 'Bill of rights, 1689' read?**

     A   William the Conqueror & Elizabeth

     B   William III (of Orange) & Mary

     C   King James II

     D   Gordon Brown

** ********

147 In the Bill of Rights in 1689, it was declared that the king or the queen must be which of these?

    A   A protestant

    B   A Roman Catholic

    C   A Puritan

    D   An Atheist

****

148 Which TWO of these were confirmed in the Bill of Rights 1689?

    A   King would no longer raise taxes or administer justice without agreement from parliament

    B   That women will have equal right to vote

    C   That a new parliament had to be elected at least every three years

    D   That women will keep their property upon marriage

****

149 Beginning of Party Politics was seen in which monarch's reign?

    A   William & Mary

    B   Victoria

    C   Queen Elizabeth II

    D   King Charles II

****

150 What were the two main groups in the parliament after 1689, when party politics started?

    A   Tories and Liberal democrats

    B   Tories & Conservatives

    C   Tories & Whigs

    D   Tories & Labour Party

****

151   When was the press freed and news papers allowed to operate without a government licence?

     A   1998

     B   1695

     C   1914

     D   55BC

****

152   What was meant by constitutional Monarchy?

     A   It meant that following Monarch's orders will be strictly a part of the constitution

     B   That Monarch will also be the prime minister

     C   That Monarchy will be ended

     D   That Monarch will not insist on matters if parliament does not agree

****

153   What were the constituencies, controlled by a single wealthy family, called?

     A   Rotten Boroughs

     B   Pocket Boroughs

     C   Round Boroughs

     D   Straight Boroughs

****

154   What were the constituencies with hardly any voters, called?

     A   Rotten Boroughs

     B   Pocket Boroughs

     C   Round Boroughs

     D   Straight Boroughs

****

155   When did the first Jews arrive in Britain?

    A   55 BC
    B   210 AD
    C   1914
    D   1656

****

156   Between 1680 and 1720, refugees came from France. What were they called?

    A   Huguenots
    B   Cavaliers
    C   Skara Brae
    D   Puritans

****

157   In 1680, why did people leave France?

    A   Because of weather
    B   Because of famine
    C   Because of Religious persecution
    D   Because of Trade

****

158   In 1707, Treaty of Union was agreed with which of the following?

    A   France
    B   Ireland
    C   Scotland
    D   Wales

****

159   Which Church does Scotland have?

    A   Cathedral

    B   Catholic

    C   Puritan

    D   Presbyterian

****

160   Who succeeded William & Mary?

    A   Queen Anne

    B   Queen Victoria

    C   Queen Elizabeth II

    D   Queen Mary

****

161   Sometime after 1714, the most important minister in the parliament became known as which of these?

    A   Prime minister

    B   Chief Minister

    C   Whip

    D   Chieftain Minister

****

162   Who succeeded Queen Anne when she died in 1714?

    A   Queen Victoria

    B   Queen Elizabeth II

    D   King George II

    D   A German - King George I

****

163   Who was the first Prime Minister of Britain?

    A   Robinhood
    B   Sir Robert Walpole
    C   Sir Francis Drake
    D   Neil Armstrong

164   When did Sir Robert become Prime Minister?

    A   1542
    B   1721
    C   1842
    D   1921

165   Bonnie Prince Charlie' was defeated by George II in Battle of Culloden. What was his real name?

    A   Charles I
    B   Robinhood
    C   Charles Edward Stuart
    D   King James

166   Which war was fought by the rebellions of the clans in Scotland?

    A   Battle of Hastings
    B   Battle of Waterloo
    C   Battle of Bannockburn
    D   Battle of Culloden

167   What happened to clansmen after the Battle of Colluden?

    A   All of them were killed
    B   They lost their children to Army
    C   They lost their lands and became tenants
    D   They became lords

****

168   Scottish landlords destroyed individual small farms. What
       was the process called?

    A   Highland Clearances
    B   Farmland Clearance

****

169   Evictions from Scotland in 19th Century led many people
       to migrate to which of these?

    A   North America
    B   Northern Ireland
    C   Scotland
    D   Russia

****

170   During the 18th century, new ideas about politics,
       philosophy and science were developed. What was this
       period called?

    A   Development
    B   Enlightenment
    C   Settlement
    D   Philosophy Age

****

171   Who was Adam Smith?

A   A Scottish known for his ideas about economics

B   A Brit known for his Culinary skills

C   An Irish painter

D   A Welsh Scientist

172   What was David Hume known for?

A   Making Steam Engine

B   Inventing Telephone

C   For his ideas about Human nature

D   For discovering penicillin

173   James Watt is known for his work on which of these?

A   Inventing Telephone

B   For his ideas about Human nature

C   For discovering penicillin

D   Work on Steam Power

174   Most important principle of Enlightenment was which of these?

A   That state can dictate what public should believe

B   That everyone has right to their own political and religious beliefs

C   That slavery have equal rights

D   That poor have equal rights

175   What was the biggest source of employment in Britain before 18th century?

        A   Agriculture
        B   Mining
        C   Slave trade
        D   Wars

****

176   There were many 'Cottage industries' where people worked from home to produce goods like which of these?

        A   Herbs & Spices
        B   Cloth & Lace
        D   Soaps
        D   Perfumes

****

177   Industrial Revolution was the rapid development of industry in Britain in which centuries?

        A   15th & 16th Centuries
        B   12th &13th Centuries
        C   18th & 19th Centuries
        D   20th & 21st Century

****

178   Large scale industrialisation in Britain happened because of which TWO of these?

        A   Development of Machinery
        B   Use of Steam Power
        C   Use of Slaves as low cost workers
        D   Vast natural resources

****

179   Britain was the first country to industrialise on a large
       scale. Is this statement true or false?

       A   True
       B   False

****

180   Bessemer Process was used for mass production of which
       of these?

       A   Steel
       B   Coal
       C   Cloth
       D   Yarn

****

181   Bessemer Process led to the development of which TWO
       of these industries?

       A   Farming
       B   Fishing
       C   Shipbuilding industry
       D   Railways

****

182   During 18th century, manufacturing jobs became the
       main source of employment in Britain. Is this statement
       true or false?

       A   True
       B   False

****

183   During the 18th century, canals were built in Britain for which TWO of these?

    A   For recreation

    B   To add beauty to landscape

    C   To link the factories to towns and cities

    D   To link the factories to ports

****

184   What were the working conditions during industrial revolution? Mark TWO answers.

    A   Very good working conditions

    B   Poor, with no laws to protect employees

    C   Employees were forced to work long hours in dangerous situations

    D   For the first time, employees were treated fairly

****

185   Children were not allowed to work during industrial revolution. Is this statement true or false?

    A   True, children's rights were a part of law and daily life

    B   False, children also worked and were sometimes treated more harshly than adults

****

186   In which TWO of these countries did the British colonisation happen in 19th century?

    A   Australia

    B   South Africa

    C   Italy

    D   Spain

****

187   Which company, originally set up to trade, gained control of large parts of India?

    A   All India Company

    B   British India Company

    C   East India Company

    D   Royal Company

****

188   What was Britain importing during industrial revolution? Mark TWO answers.

    A   Sugar & Tobacco

    B   Textile

    C   Planes

    D   Weapons

****

189   By which century slavery was a fully established overseas industry?

    A   12th century

    B   14th century

    C   18th Century

    D   20th century

****

190   Slaves primarily came from which country?

    A   West Africa

    B   North America

    C   East India

    D   Vietnam

****

191   **British ships used to take slaves to which TWO of these countries?**

    A   India

    B   Australia

    C   America

    D   Caribbean

****

192   **Who set up the first formal anti-slavery groups in the late 1700s?**

    A   The Quakers

    B   The Quangos

    C   The Rebellious Clans

    D   The Roman Catholics

****

193   **The slave trade was flourishing well till 1933. Is this statement true or false?**

    A   True

    B   False

****

194   **When did it become illegal to trade slaves in British ships or from British ports?**

    A   1700

    B   1210

    C   1807

    D   1990

****

195   When did the Emancipation Act abolished slavery throughout the British empire?

    A   1700

    B   1210

    C   1807

    D   1833

196   After slave trade was abolished, 2 million people from which countries were employed to replace the freed slaves?

    A   India & China

    B   Thailand and Vietnam

    C   Canada & Australia

    D   Ireland & Scotland

197   Why had many of the colonist families originally gone to North America?

    A   To make wealth

    B   To avoid taxes

    C   To fight

    D   To have religious freedom

198   When did the American colonies declare independence from Britain?

    A   1876

    B   1895

    C   1707

    D   1776

199   When did Britain recognise the independence of American colonies?

    A   1990

    B   1914

    C   1783

    D   1200

200   Britain's navy fought against combined French and Spanish fleets in 1805. What was the battle called?

    A   Battle of Trafalgar

    B   Battle of Hastings

    C   Battle of Bannockburn

    D   Battle of Waterloo

201   Who defeated the French Emperor Napoleon in 1815?

    A   William the Conqueror

    B   Duke of Wellington

    C   William Shakespeare

    D   Tony Blair

202   In which battle was the French Emperor Napoleon defeated in 1815?

    A   Battle of Trafalgar

    B   Battle of Hastings

    C   Battle of Bannockburn

    D   Battle of Waterloo

203   Queen Victoria, became queen in 1837 and ruled UK for how many years?

     A   14
     B   20
     C   64
     D   100

****

204   British Empire was the largest the world had ever seen. What was the estimated population?

     A   4 million
     B   400 million
     C   4 billion
     D   100 million

****

205   What is the period of reign of Queen Victoria called?

     A   Victoria's period
     B   Victoria's time
     C   Victorian Age
     D   Age of Power

****

206   Between 1853 and 1913, how many British citizens left the country?

     A   100 thousand
     B   1 million
     C   10 million
     D   13 million

****

207   Between 1870 and 1914, around 120,000 Jews came to Britain. Which TWO countries did they come from?

      A   Russia

      B   Saudi Arabia

      C   India

      D   Poland

****

208   Just before Victoria came to the throne, which of these pioneered the railway engine?

      A   Richard Arkwright

      B   Isambard Kingdom Brunel

      C   The father and son George and Robert Stephenson

      D   Isaac Newton

****

209   Major expansion of the railways took place in the era of which of these?

      A   Victoria

      B   Charles I

      C   King James II

      D   Winston Churchill

****

210   In 19th century, UK was responsible for more than half of the worlds' produce of which TWO of these?

      A   Iron

      B   Spices

      C   Coal

      D   Salt

****

211   In 19th century, UK also became a centre for financial
       services, including which TWO of these?

              A   Banking
              B   Insurance
              C   International mortgages
              D   Leasing

212   In 1851, the Great Exhibition opened in Hyde Park, for
       goods and machines made in which countries?

              A   All over Britain
              B   Countries all over the world

213   The Crimean War was fought against which of these
       countries?

              A   Turkey
              B   France
              C   Russia
              D   America

214   Victorian Cross Medal was introduced to acknowledge
       which of these?

              A   Religious Strength
              B   Trade Skills
              C   Acts of valour in war
              D   Human Rights

215 A million people died in Ireland in mid 19th century. What were the reasons? Mark TWO correct answers.

    A   Potato crop failed & caused famine
    B   Religious clashes
    C   People died of diseases and starvation
    D   Irish Nationalist Movement

****

216 Regarding Irish nationalist movement, which of these favoured complete independence and not the home rule?

    A   Fenians
    B   Others like Charles Stuart Parnell

****

217 What did the Reform Act of 1832 do? Mark TWO correct answers.

    A   Increased the number of people with right to vote
    B   Abolished the old pocket and rotten boroughs
    C   Abolished Monarchy
    D   Gave Women the right to vote

****

218 What was the demand of campaigners called the Chartists?

    A   Vote for working classes
    B   Reduced powers for pope
    C   Reduced powers for king
    D   Seats in House of Lords

****

219   Reform Act of 1867 gave women the right to vote. Is this statement true or false?

    A   True
    B   False

****

220   What does Universal Suffrage mean?

    A   Right of men to vote
    B   Right of women to vote
    C   Right of every adult, male or female, to vote
    D   Right of labour class to vote

****

221   Until which year did the earnings, property and money of a woman automatically belonged to her husband upon marriage?

    A   1945
    B   1715
    C   1870
    D   2006

****

222   In late 19th century, women demonstrated for their rights to vote. What were these women called?

    A   Suffragettes
    B   Rebellions
    C   Puritan
    D   Enthusiasts

****

223   British Empire continued to grow until which year?

    A   2001
    B   1850
    C   1902
    D   1920

224   Boers' with whom Britain went to war in South Africa, were settlers from which of these countries?

    A   Scotland
    B   Netherlands
    C   Australia
    D   America

225   Early 20th century was a time of optimism in Britain. What important measures were introduced? Mark TWO answers.

    A   Free school meals
    B   Pensions and benefits
    C   New taxes were introduced
    D   No one had to pay tax

226   When did the First World War start?

    A   1914
    B   1980
    C   1947
    D   1800

227   Which TWO factors were responsible for the First World War? Mark TWO correct answers.

     A   Imperialism
     B   Militarism
     C   Religious extremism
     D   Terrorism

****

228   Which of these countries were among the allied forces in the First World war?

     A   Britain, France, Russia & Japan
     B   Britain, France, Italy & Germany

****

229   When did the First World War end?

     A   1914
     B   1918
     C   1947
     D   1980

****

230   In which year did British government promise Home Rule for Ireland?

     A   1913
     B   1916
     C   1921
     D   1922

****

231   When did Ireland become two countries?

     A   1922
     B   1850
     C   1947
     D   2002

232 When did BBC start its radio broadcasts?

    A   1922

    B   1850

    C   1947

    D   2002

233 Part of Ireland under UK is mainly of which religious group?

    A   Catholics

    B   Protestants

    C   Atheists

    D   Puritans

234 When did the world enter the 'Great Depression'?

    A   2008

    B   2012

    C   1914

    D   1930

235 What were the new industries in Britain in 1930s?

    A   Shipbuilding & boats

    B   Automobile & Aviation

    C   Coal Mining

    D   Textiles

236   In 1936, BBC began which of the world's first regular service?

    A   Stage Shows

    B   Radio

    C   Television

    D   iPlayer

237   Adolf Hitler came to power in 1933 in which of these countries?

    A   UK

    B   France

    C   Scotland

    D   Germany

238   Who were the Axis Powers in 2nd World War?

    A   Germany, Italy & Japan

    B   France, Russia & Japan

    C   France, Russia & America

    D   America & Japan

239   Which of these were among the Allied Countries in 2nd World War?

    A   Germany, Italy & Japan

    B   France, Russia & Japan

    C   UK, France, Canada

    D   America & Japan

240   In 1940, Allied troops defeated German forces and won the war. Is this statement true or false?

    A   True

    B   False

****

241   The phrase, 'Dunkirk spirit' is a reminder of how which of these took place during 2nd World War?

    A   60,000 British troops fought to death in Dunkirk

    B   300,000 British & French troops were rescued from Dunkirk

****

242   Who was the British Prime Minister during the 2nd World War?

    A   William of Orange

    B   Tony Blair

    C   Margaret Thatcher

    D   Winston Churchill

****

243   The Royal Air force used which of these British made planes to win the Battle of Britain against Germany?

    A   Spitfire & Hurricane

    B   Thunder & Wonder

    C   F16 & C130

    D   Concorde & Titanic

****

244   What was the bombing of London and other British cities by Germans called?

    A   Terrorism
    B   Blitz
    C   Blasts
    D   Thunders

245   Which American Naval Base was attacked by the Japanese?

    A   Vietnam
    B   Qatar
    C   Bahrain
    D   Pearl Harbour

246   When did the United States drop its atom bombs on the Japanese cities of Hiroshima and Nagasaki?

    A   1980
    B   2003
    C   1945
    D   1947

247   What does NHS stand for?

    A   National Health Security
    B   National Health Server
    C   National Health Service
    D   National Health Scheme

248   When was NHS established?

    A   In 1941, under Winston Churchill's government

    B   In 1948, under Labour government

****

249   Nine countries including Pakistan & India were granted independence from Britain in which year?

    A   1850

    B   1875

    C   1945

    D   1947

****

250   In 1948 and during 1950's, people from West Indies were recruited for which jobs?

    A   Show business

    B   Cooking

    C   Driving Buses

    D   Construction

****

251   During 1950's, people from India & Pakistan were recruited for which jobs? Mark TWO correct answers.

    A   Textiles

    B   Engineering

    C   Driving Buses

    D   Growing potatoes

****

252   The Swinging Sixties [1960's] are well known for which of these? Mark TWO correct answers.

    A   Wars

    B   Cinema & Music

    C   Fashion

    D   Poverty

253   When did it become illegal for employers to discriminate against women because of their gender?

    A   1960's

    B   1940's

    C   1980's

    D   1900's

254   The world's only supersonic commercial airliner, Concorde was made in 1960. Which countries made it?

    A   Britain

    B   Britain & France

    C   America

    D   America & Japan

255   In 1960's less people migrated to UK. What was the reason?

    A   Continuous wars

    B   They were not paid enough

    C   Immigration controls got stricter

    D   People were afraid of IRA

256   Why did Britain admit 28,000 people of Indian origin in 1970s?

    A   They were forced to leave Uganda

    B   Britain needed bus drivers

    C   Britain needed doctors

    D   They were returning slaves from the Empire

257 The 1970s were also a time of serious unrest in which of these countries?

    A   Scotland

    B   Wales

    C   France

    D   Northern Ireland

****

258 When did European Economic Community come into being?

    A   1914

    B   1945

    C   1957

    D   1970

****

259 The Labour party privatised the main nationalised industries and public services. Is this statement true of false?

    A   True

    B   False

****

260 Tony Blair got elected in 2007. Which TWO of the following happened in his government?

    A   Scottish Parliament was formed

    B   Britain invented Concorde

    C   Good Friday Agreement signed with Ireland, due to peace process, in 1998

    D   Penicillin was discovered

****

261 In the 1990s, Britain played a leading role in coalition forces involved in the liberation of which of these countries?

    A   Saudi Arabia

    B   France

    C   Kuwait

    D   Iraq

****

262 When did British Armed Forces leave Iraq?

    A   2012

    B   2011

    C   2009

    D   2004

****

263 British troops are in Afghanistan as a part of which international organisation?

    A   ISAF

    B   NATO

    C   WHO

    D   UNICEF

****

264 In which year will Afghan National Security Forces will have full security responsibility handed over by ISAF troops?

    A   2020

    B   2010

    C   2014

    D   2013

****

265   Present day government in UK is run by which of these?

A   A conservative government

B   A Labour Party government

C   A coalition between Conservative Party & Liberal Democrats

D   A coalition between Labour & Liberal Democrats

****

266   How many wives did Henry VIII have?

A   12

B   2

C   1

D   6

****

267   Which TWO of these are true about Henry VIII's first wife?

A   She was Catherine of Aragon

B   She was a German Princess

C   She was a Spanish Princess

D   She was executed for taking lovers

*** ************************

268   Which of the following Henry VIII's wives was executed at Tower of London?

A   Catherine of Aragon

B   Anne Boleyn

C   Jane Seymour

D   Anne of Cleves

*** ***********************

269   Where was Shakespeare born?

A   Birmingham

B   London

C   Manchester

D   Stratford-upon-Avon

270   Shakespeare's writings focussed solely on kings and Queens. Is this statement true or false?

    A   True
    B   False

271   The darling buds of May' is a line from whose sonnet?

    A   William Wordsworth
    B   William Shakespeare
    C   Robert Burns
    D   Henry Fielding

272   To be or not to be' is a line from which play of William Shakespeare?

    A   Hamlet
    B   As you like it
    C   Romeo & Juliet
    D   A Midsummer Night Dream

273   Which of these is correct about the King James' Bible?

    A   It was the first English bible
    B   It is a version which continues to be used in many protestant Churches today

274   Who discovered that white light is made up of the colours of rainbow?

    A   William Shakespeare
    B   Graham Bell
    C   Isaac Newton
    D   Tony Blair

275   Who was Sir Isaac Newton?

    A   A member of house of Lords

    B   A Beatles' Singer

    C   A Knight

    D   A renowned Scientist

276   Who was Robert Burns?

    A   A Scottish poet

    B   An English Politician

    C   A French Chef

    D   An Irish Politician

277   Richard Arkwright [1732-92] used steam engine to power machinery. Is this statement true or false?

    A   False

    B   True

278   Sake Dean Mahomet [1759-1851], introduced which of the following to Britain?

    A   Indian Sword Fighting Skills

    B   Urdu Language

    C   The Indian head massage called 'Shampooing'

    D   Indian Curry

279   When did the 'Act of Union' (with Ireland) pass?

    A   1782

    B   1541

    C   1821

    D   1800

****

280   When did Ireland become unified with England, Scotland & Wales?

        A   1801
        B   1914
        C   1920
        D   2002

****

281   What is the official flag of UK called?

        A   Union James
        B   Union Jack
        C   Flag of all Saints
        D   Flag of Unity

****

282   Which of these crosses represents St George of England on UK Flag?

        A   A red cross on a white ground
        B   A diagonal white cross on a blue ground
        C   A diagonal red cross on a white ground
        D   A white cross on red ground

****

283   What is printed on the official Welsh flag?

        A   A Welsh Dragon
        B   A Welsh Butterfly
        C   A Welsh Monument
        D   A Welsh Poppy

****

284   The Great Western Railway were constructed by which engineer known for building other tunnels, bridges and railway lines etc?

     A   Robert Wallace

     B   Isambard Brunel

     C   Robert Burns

     D   Isaac Newton

****

285   Florence Nightingale treated soldiers in which of these wars?

     A   Crimean

     B   World War 1

     C   World War II

     D   War of Roses

****

286   In 1860 Florence Nightingale established the Nightingale Training School for nurses in which of these places?

     A   Paris

     B   London

     C   Germany

     D   Italy

****

287   Who was Emmeline Pankhurst?

     A   A women's right activist

     B   A poetess

     C   A Scientist

     D   Writer of Harry Potter

****

288   In which year women were given the right to vote at 21, that is at the same age as men?

    A   1925
    B   1927
    C   1928
    D   1935

289   Who were Suffragettes?

    A   Women who took part in First World War
    B   Women campaigning for rights of women
    C   Women workers in factories
    D   Women members of parliament

290   Which of the following statements is correct?

    A   The 'suffragettes' used civil disobedience, chained themselves, smashed windows and committed arson to fight for women rights.
    B   The 'suffragettes' used civil disobedience, chained themselves, smashed windows and killed animals to fight for women rights.

291   Which TWO of these statements are correct?

    A   Rudyard Kipling was awarded Nobel prize in 1990
    B   Rudyard Kipling wrote 'The Jungle Book'
    C   Rudyard Kipling was born in India
    D   Rudyard Kipling was also an actor

292   Which TWO are correct about Winston Churchill?

     A   He was a Conservative Prime Minister

     B   He was a Labour MP

     C   He was a journalist

     D   He was an Oscar winning actor

****

293   Winston Churchill died in 1965 and received a state funeral. Is this statement true or false?

     A   True

     B   False

****

294   Who discovered penicillin?

     A   Graham Bell

     B   Alexander Fleming

     C   Sir Isaac Newton

     D   William Wordsworth

****

295   Who was Clement Attlee?

     A   A labour Prime Minister who introduced NHS

     B   Leader of Liberal democrats in 70's

     C   A conservative MP

     D   Leader of Suffrage movement

****

296   Who recommended that government should find ways of fighting the five 'Giant Evils' of Want, Disease, Ignorance, Squalor and Idleness?

     A   RA Butler

     B   Dylan Thomas

     C   William Beveridge

     D   Winston Churchill

297   Who introduced the Education Act 1944?

    A   RA Butler
    B   Dylan Thomas
    C   William Beveridge
    D   Rudyard Kipling

298   After which Act or Bill was free secondary education introduced in UK?

    A   After Butler Act in 1944
    B   After Act of Union 1800
    C   After Bill of Rights 1869
    D   After European Convention on Human Rights in 2000

299   Which TWO of these were famously written by Dylan Thomas?

    A   The radio play 'Under Milk Wood'
    B   Good Bye Mr Kipling
    C   The Poem: Do Not Go Gentle into That Good Night
    D   Charlie & The Chocolate Factory

300   Television is a French invention. Is this statement true or false?

    A   True
    B   False

301   **Which TWO of these were invented by Scottish Scientists?**

      A   Television

      B   Radar

      C   Turing Machine

      D   Hovercraft

****

302   **Which TWO of these inventions are British?**

      A   Playstation

      B   World Wide Web

      C   Jet Engine

      D   CD Player

****

303   **Which of these is true about the Harrier Jump Jet?**

      A   The world's only supersonic passenger aircraft

      B   An aircraft, designed and developed in UK, capable of taking off vertically

****

304   **Which of these is true about the Concorde?**

      A   The world's only supersonic passenger aircraft, developed by France and Britain

      B   An aircraft, designed and developed in UK, capable of taking off vertically

****

305   **IVF (In-vitro fertilisation) therapy for treatment of infertility was pioneered in Britain. Is this statement true or false?**

      A   True

      B   False

306   Two British Scientists were the first to succeed in cloning a sheep. What was the sheep named?

A   Molly the sheep

B   Dolly the sheep

C   Woolly the sheep

D   Shelly the Dolly

307   Who invented the cash dispensing ATM (automatic teller machine) or 'cashpoint?

A   Sir Tim Berners-Lee

B   Sir Robert Walpole

C   Sir Robert Edwards

D   James Goodfellow

308   The first of cash dispensing ATM (automatic teller machine) or 'cashpoint was used by which bank in UK?

A   NatWest

B   Halifax

C   Barclays

D   HSBC

309   Who was the inventor of the World Wide Web?

A   Sir Tim Berners-Lee

B   Sir Robert Walpole

C   Sir Robert Edwards

D   Sir Frank Whittle

310   Who developed the Jet Engine?

    A   Sir Tim Berners-Lee

    B   Sir Robert Walpole

    C   Sir Robert Edwards

    D   Sir Frank Whittle

****

311   Who invented hovercraft?

    A   Sir Christopher Cockerell

    B   James Goodfellow

    C   Sir Robert Edwards

    D   Sir Frank Whittle

****

312   Which of these athletes won an Olympic gold medal in the pentathlon in 1972?

    A   Mo Farah

    B   Bradley Wiggins

    C   Dame Ellen MacArthur

    D   Jessica Ennis

****

313   Which athlete was made a Dame of the British Empire in 2000 in recognition of her work to promote sports in Northern Ireland?

    A   Dame Judy Dench

    B   Dame Helen Mirren

    C   Dame May Peters

    D   Dame Ellen MacArthur

****

314   Margaret Thatcher was the daughter of a grocer from Grantham in Lincolnshire. Is this statement true or false?

    A   True
    B   False

315   In which year was Margaret Thatcher elected as the leader of the Conservative party?

    A   1925
    B   1959
    C   1970
    D   1975

316   In 1970, Margaret Thatcher became a secretary of state for which of these?

    A   Defence
    B   Foreign Affairs
    C   Education & Science
    D   Health

317   In 1979, Margaret Thatcher became the first woman prime minister of the UK. Is this statement true or false?

    A   True
    B   False

318   Who was the longest serving prime minister of the 20th century?

    A   Tony Blair
    B   Margaret Thatcher
    C   Winston Churchill
    D   Clement Attlee

****

319   Who wrote 'Charlie & the Chocolate Factory'?

    A   Mary Peters

    B   Dylan Thomas

    C   Roald Dahl

    D   William Blake

****

320   Which of these served in Royal Air force during 2nd World War?

    A   Mary Peters

    B   Dylan Thomas

    C   Roald Dahl

    D   William Blake

****

321   In year 55 BC, what does BC refer to?

    A   Before Christmas

    B   Before Christ

****

322   In year 410 AD, what does AD refer to?

    A   Anno Domini- that is years after birth of Jesus Christ

    B   After Death of Jesus Christ

****

ANSWER KEY

| Q.# | Answer | Reference | |
		Chapter	Page No.
1.	D	A long & illustrious history	p. 15
2.	C	A long & illustrious history	p. 15
3.	C	A long & illustrious history	p. 15
4.	C	A long & illustrious history	p. 15
5.	D	A long & illustrious history	p. 15
6.	C	A long & illustrious history	p. 15
7.	C	A long & illustrious history	p. 15
8.	A	A long & illustrious history	p. 15
9.	C	A long & illustrious history	p. 15
10.	D	A long & illustrious history	p. 16
11.	C	A long & illustrious history	p. 15
12.	B	A long & illustrious history	p. 16
13.	A	A long & illustrious history	p. 16
14.	B	A long & illustrious history	p. 16
15.	C	A long & illustrious history	p. 16
16.	D	A long & illustrious history	p. 16
17.	A	A long & illustrious history	p. 16
18.	C	A long & illustrious history	p. 16
19.	A	A long & illustrious history	p. 16
20.	C	A long & illustrious history	p. 16
21.	A	A long & illustrious history	p. 17
22.	B	A long & illustrious history	p. 17

ANSWER KEY

Q.#	Answer	Reference	
		Chapter	Page No.
23.	C	A long & illustrious history	p. 17
24.	A & B	A long & illustrious history	p. 17
25.	C	A long & illustrious history	p. 17
26.	A	A long & illustrious history	p. 17
27.	D	A long & illustrious history	p. 17
28.	D	A long & illustrious history	p. 17
29.	A & D	A long & illustrious history	p. 17
30.	B	A long & illustrious history	p. 17
31.	B	A long & illustrious history	p. 17
32.	C	A long & illustrious history	p. 17
33.	A & C	A long & illustrious history	p. 17
34.	C	A long & illustrious history	p. 17
35.	D	A long & illustrious history	p. 17
36.	A	A long & illustrious history	p. 18
37.	A	A long & illustrious history	p. 18
38.	C	A long & illustrious history	p. 19
39.	B	A long & illustrious history	p. 19
40.	B & D	A long & illustrious history	p. 19
41.	C	A long & illustrious history	p. 19
42.	C	A long & illustrious history	p. 19
43.	B & C	A long & illustrious history	p. 19
44.	A	A long & illustrious history	p. 19

ANSWER KEY

Q.#	Answer	Reference	
		Chapter	Page No.
45.	A	A long & illustrious history	p. 19
46.	B	A long & illustrious history	p. 19
47.	D	A long & illustrious history	p. 19
48.	B	A long & illustrious history	p. 19
49.	A	A long & illustrious history	p. 19
50.	C	A long & illustrious history	p. 19
51.	A	A long & illustrious history	p. 20
52.	B	A long & illustrious history	p. 20
53.	A & B	A long & illustrious history	p. 20
54.	C	A long & illustrious history	p. 21
55.	A	A long & illustrious history	p. 21
56.	C	A long & illustrious history	p. 21
57.	C	A long & illustrious history	p. 21
58.	B	A long & illustrious history	p. 21
59.	D	A long & illustrious history	p. 21
60.	B	A long & illustrious history	p. 21
61.	B	A long & illustrious history	p. 21
62.	A	A long & illustrious history	p. 21
63.	C	A long & illustrious history	p. 21
64.	A	A long & illustrious history	p. 21
65.	B	A long & illustrious history	p. 21
66.	D	A long & illustrious history	p. 21

ANSWER KEY

Q.#	Answer	Reference	
		Chapter	Page No.
67.	C	A long & illustrious history	p. 22
68.	C	A long & illustrious history	p. 22
69.	A	A long & illustrious history	p. 22
70.	D	A long & illustrious history	p. 22
71.	A	A long & illustrious history	p. 22
72.	B	A long & illustrious history	p. 22
73.	C	A long & illustrious history	p. 22
74.	A	A long & illustrious history	p. 22
75.	A	A long & illustrious history	p. 22
76.	D	A long & illustrious history	p. 22
77.	B	A long & illustrious history	p. 22
78.	A & C	A long & illustrious history	p. 23
79.	A & D	A long & illustrious history	p. 23
80.	B	A long & illustrious history	p. 23
81.	C	A long & illustrious history	p. 23
82.	A	A long & illustrious history	p. 23
83.	A	A long & illustrious history	p. 23
84.	A & D	A long & illustrious history	p. 23
85.	B	A long & illustrious history	p. 23
86.	C	A long & illustrious history	p. 23-24
87.	D	A long & illustrious history	p. 24
88.	B	A long & illustrious history	p. 24

ANSWER KEY

Q.#	Answer	Reference	
		Chapter	Page No.
89.	A & B	A long & illustrious history	p. 24
90.	C	A long & illustrious history	p. 24
91.	C & D	A long & illustrious history	p. 24
92.	A & B	A long & illustrious history	p. 25
93.	B	A long & illustrious history	p. 25
94.	C	A long & illustrious history	p. 25
95.	A	A long & illustrious history	p. 25
96.	D	A long & illustrious history	p. 25
97.	B	A long & illustrious history	p. 25
98.	A	A long & illustrious history	p. 25
99.	C	A long & illustrious history	p. 25
100.	C	A long & illustrious history	p. 27
101.	A	A long & illustrious history	p. 27
102.	A	A long & illustrious history	p. 27
103.	B	A long & illustrious history	p. 27
104.	C	A long & illustrious history	p. 27
105.	A	A long & illustrious history	p. 27
106.	A	A long & illustrious history	p. 27
107.	C	A long & illustrious history	p. 28
108.	B	A long & illustrious history	p. 28
109.	D	A long & illustrious history	p. 28
110.	C	A long & illustrious history	p. 28

ANSWER KEY

Q.#	Answer	Reference	
		Chapter	Page No.
111.	A	A long & illustrious history	p. 29
112.	A	A long & illustrious history	p. 28
113.	B	A long & illustrious history	p. 29
114.	B	A long & illustrious history	p. 29
115.	A	A long & illustrious history	p. 29
116.	B	A long & illustrious history	p. 29
117.	C	A long & illustrious history	p. 29
118.	B	A long & illustrious history	p. 29
119.	A & C	A long & illustrious history	p. 29
120.	C	A long & illustrious history	p. 29
121.	C	A long & illustrious history	p. 30
122.	B	A long & illustrious history	p. 31
123.	B & C	A long & illustrious history	p. 31
124.	D	A long & illustrious history	p. 31
125.	A	A long & illustrious history	p. 31
126.	A	A long & illustrious history	p. 32
127.	B	A long & illustrious history	p. 33
128.	C	A long & illustrious history	p. 33
129.	D	A long & illustrious history	p. 33
130.	A	A long & illustrious history	p. 33-34
131.	C	A long & illustrious history	p. 34
132.	D	A long & illustrious history	p. 34

ANSWER KEY

Q.#	Answer	Reference	
		Chapter	Page No.
133.	C	A long & illustrious history	p. 34
134.	D	A long & illustrious history	p. 34
135.	A	A long & illustrious history	p. 34
136.	A & B	A long & illustrious history	p. 35
137.	A	A long & illustrious history	p. 35
138.	D	A long & illustrious history	p. 35
139.	B	A long & illustrious history	p. 35
140.	C	A long & illustrious history	p. 35
141.	A	A long & illustrious history	p. 36
142.	D	A long & illustrious history	p. 36
143.	A	A long & illustrious history	p. 36
144.	B	A long & illustrious history	p. 36
145.	C	A long & illustrious history	p. 37
146.	B	A long & illustrious history	p. 37
147.	A	A long & illustrious history	p. 37
148.	A & C	A long & illustrious history	p. 37
149.	A	A long & illustrious history	p. 37
150.	C	A long & illustrious history	p. 37
151.	B	A long & illustrious history	p. 38
152.	D	A long & illustrious history	p. 38
153.	B	A long & illustrious history	p. 38
154.	A	A long & illustrious history	p. 38

ANSWER KEY

Q.#	Answer	Reference	
		Chapter	Page No.
155.	D	A long & illustrious history	p. 38
156.	A	A long & illustrious history	p. 38
157.	C	A long & illustrious history	p. 38
158.	C	A long & illustrious history	p. 38
159.	D	A long & illustrious history	p. 38
160.	A	A long & illustrious history	p. 38
161.	A	A long & illustrious history	p. 39
162.	D	A long & illustrious history	p. 39
163.	B	A long & illustrious history	p. 39
164.	B	A long & illustrious history	p. 39
165.	C	A long & illustrious history	p. 39
166.	D	A long & illustrious history	p. 39
167.	C	A long & illustrious history	p. 39
168.	A	A long & illustrious history	p. 39
169.	A	A long & illustrious history	p. 39
170.	B	A long & illustrious history	p. 40
171.	A	A long & illustrious history	p. 40
172.	C	A long & illustrious history	p. 40
173.	D	A long & illustrious history	p. 40
174.	B	A long & illustrious history	p. 40
175.	A	A long & illustrious history	p. 40
176.	B	A long & illustrious history	p. 40

ANSWER KEY

Q.#	Answer	Reference	
		Chapter	Page No.
177.	C	A long & illustrious history	p. 40
178.	A & B	A long & illustrious history	p. 40
179.	A	A long & illustrious history	p. 40
180.	A	A long & illustrious history	p. 41
181.	C & D	A long & illustrious history	p. 41
182.	A	A long & illustrious history	p. 41
183.	C & D	A long & illustrious history	p. 42
184.	B & C	A long & illustrious history	p. 42
185.	B	A long & illustrious history	p. 42
186.	A & B	A long & illustrious history	p. 42
187.	C	A long & illustrious history	p. 42
188.	A & B	A long & illustrious history	p. 42
189.	C	A long & illustrious history	p. 43
190.	A	A long & illustrious history	p. 43
191.	C & D	A long & illustrious history	p. 43
192.	A	A long & illustrious history	p. 43
193.	B	A long & illustrious history	p. 43
194.	C	A long & illustrious history	p. 43
195.	D	A long & illustrious history	p. 43
196.	A	A long & illustrious history	p. 43
197.	D	A long & illustrious history	p. 43
198.	D	A long & illustrious history	p. 44

ANSWER KEY

Q.#	Answer	Reference	
		Chapter	Page No.
199.	C	A long & illustrious history	p. 44
200.	A	A long & illustrious history	p. 44
201.	B	A long & illustrious history	p. 44
202.	D	A long & illustrious history	p. 44
203.	C	A long & illustrious history	p. 47
204.	B	A long & illustrious history	p. 47
205.	C	A long & illustrious history	p. 47
206.	D	A long & illustrious history	p. 47
207.	A & D	A long & illustrious history	p. 47
208.	C	A long & illustrious history	p. 48
209.	A	A long & illustrious history	p. 48
210.	A & C	A long & illustrious history	p. 49
211.	A & B	A long & illustrious history	p. 49
212.	B	A long & illustrious history	p. 49
213.	C	A long & illustrious history	p. 49
214.	C	A long & illustrious history	p. 49
215.	A & C	A long & illustrious history	p. 49
216.	A	A long & illustrious history	p. 50
217.	A & B	A long & illustrious history	p. 50
218.	A	A long & illustrious history	p. 50
219.	B	A long & illustrious history	p. 50
220.	C	A long & illustrious history	p. 50

ANSWER KEY

Q.#	Answer	Reference	
		Chapter	Page No.
221.	C	A long & illustrious history	p. 50
222.	A	A long & illustrious history	p. 50-51
223.	D	A long & illustrious history	p. 51
224.	B	A long & illustrious history	p. 51
225.	A & B	A long & illustrious history	p. 53
226.	A	A long & illustrious history	p. 54
227.	A & B	A long & illustrious history	p. 54
228.	A	A long & illustrious history	p. 54
229.	B	A long & illustrious history	p. 55
230.	A	A long & illustrious history	p. 55
231.	A	A long & illustrious history	p. 55
232.	A	A long & illustrious history	p. 56
233.	B	A long & illustrious history	p. 55
234.	D	A long & illustrious history	p. 55
235.	B	A long & illustrious history	p. 55
236.	C	A long & illustrious history	p. 56
237.	D	A long & illustrious history	p. 56
238.	A	A long & illustrious history	p. 56
239.	C	A long & illustrious history	p. 56
240.	B	A long & illustrious history	p. 56
241.	B	A long & illustrious history	p. 58
242.	D	A long & illustrious history	p. 56

ANSWER KEY

Q.#	Answer	Reference	
		Chapter	Page No.
243.	A	A long & illustrious history	p. 58
244.	B	A long & illustrious history	p. 58
245.	D	A long & illustrious history	p. 58
246.	C	A long & illustrious history	p. 59
247.	C	A long & illustrious history	p. 60
248.	B	A long & illustrious history	p. 60
249.	D	A long & illustrious history	p. 61
250.	C	A long & illustrious history	p. 63
251.	A & B	A long & illustrious history	p. 63
252.	B & C	A long & illustrious history	p. 63
253.	A	A long & illustrious history	p. 63
254.	B	A long & illustrious history	p. 63
255.	C	A long & illustrious history	p. 64
256.	A	A long & illustrious history	p. 64
257.	D	A long & illustrious history	p. 66
258.	C	A long & illustrious history	p. 66
259.	B	A long & illustrious history	p. 67
260.	A & C	A long & illustrious history	p. 68
261.	C	A long & illustrious history	p. 68
262.	C	A long & illustrious history	p. 68
263.	A	A long & illustrious history	p. 68
264.	C	A long & illustrious history	p. 69

ANSWER KEY

| Q.# | Answer | Reference | |
		Chapter	Page No.
265.	C	A long & illustrious history	p. 69
266.	D	A long & illustrious history	p. 27-Box
267.	A & C	A long & illustrious history	p. 27-Box
268.	B	A long & illustrious history	p. 27-Box
269.	D	A long & illustrious history	p. 30-Box
270.	B	A long & illustrious history	p. 30-Box
271.	B	A long & illustrious history	p. 30-Box
272.	A	A long & illustrious history	p. 30-Box
273.	B	A long & illustrious history	p. 31-Box
274.	C	A long & illustrious history	p. 35-Box
275.	D	A long & illustrious history	p. 35-Box
276.	A	A long & illustrious history	p. 40-Box
277.	B	A long & illustrious history	p. 41-Box
278.	C & D	A long & illustrious history	p. 42-Box
279.	D	A long & illustrious history	p. 45-Box
280.	A	A long & illustrious history	p. 45-Box
281.	B	A long & illustrious history	p. 45-Box
282.	A	A long & illustrious history	p. 45-Box
283.	A	A long & illustrious history	p. 45-Box
284.	B	A long & illustrious history	p. 48-Box
285.	A	A long & illustrious history	p. 49-Box
286.	B	A long & illustrious history	p. 49-Box

ANSWER KEY

Q.#	Answer	Reference	
		Chapter	Page No.
287.	A	A long & illustrious history	p. 51-Box
288.	C	A long & illustrious history	p. 51-Box
289.	B	A long & illustrious history	p. 51-Box
290.	A	A long & illustrious history	p. 51-Box
291.	B & C	A long & illustrious history	p. 52-Box
292.	A & C	A long & illustrious history	p. 56-Box
293.	A	A long & illustrious history	p. 56-Box
294.	B	A long & illustrious history	p. 60-Box
295.	A	A long & illustrious history	p. 61-Box
296.	C	A long & illustrious history	p. 62-Box
297.	A	A long & illustrious history	p. 62-Box
298.	A	A long & illustrious history	p. 62-Box
299.	A & C	A long & illustrious history	p. 62-Box
300.	B	A long & illustrious history	p. 64-Box
301.	A & B	A long & illustrious history	p. 65-Box
302.	B & C	A long & illustrious history	p. 65-Box
303.	B	A long & illustrious history	p. 65-Box
304.	A	A long & illustrious history	p. 65-Box
305.	A	A long & illustrious history	p. 65-Box
306.	B	A long & illustrious history	p. 65-Box
307.	D	A long & illustrious history	p. 65-Box
308.	C	A long & illustrious history	p. 65-Box

ANSWER KEY

Q.#	Answer	Reference	
		Chapter	Page No.
309.	A	A long & illustrious history	p. 65-Box
310.	D	A long & illustrious history	p. 65-Box
311.	A	A long & illustrious history	p. 65-Box
312.	C	A long & illustrious history	p. 66-Box
313.	D	A long & illustrious history	p. 66-Box
314.	A	A long & illustrious history	p. 67-Box
315.	D	A long & illustrious history	p. 67-Box
316.	C	A long & illustrious history	p. 67-Box
317.	A	A long & illustrious history	p. 67-Box
318.	B	A long & illustrious history	p. 67-Box
319.	C	A long & illustrious history	p. 68-Box
320.	C	A long & illustrious history	p. 68-Box
321.	B	A long & illustrious history	p. 17
322.	A	A long & illustrious history	p. 17

Chapter 4:

A Modern Thriving Society

1   Approximately what % of the population has a parent or
        grandparent born outside the UK?

        A   50
        B   40
        C   20
        D   10

2   What is the longest distance on UK mainland?

        A   2000 miles
        B   1000 miles
        C   870 miles
        D   400 miles

3   Which city is the capital of UK?

        A   London
        B   Liverpool
        C   Manchester
        D   Oxford

4   Which is the capital of Scotland?

        A   Glasgow
        B   London
        C   Edinburgh
        D   Dundee

5   Which is the capital of Wales?

        A   Glasgow
        B   Belfast
        C   Newcastle Upon Tyne
        D   Cardiff

6   Which is the capital of Northern Ireland?

    A   Belfast
    B   Aberdeen
    C   Pale
    D   Dublin

7   Which TWO of these are in Wales?

    A   Aberdeen
    B   Cardiff
    C   Oxford
    D   Swansea

8   Which TWO of these are in Scotland?

    A   Aberdeen
    B   Snowdonia
    C   Dumfries
    D   Dundee

9   Which TWO of these are in Northern Ireland?

    A   Cornwall
    B   Dundee
    C   Belfast
    D   Birmingham

10   Which TWO of these are in England?

    A   Dumfries
    B   Norwich
    C   Snowdonia
    D   Bradford

****

11 Plymouth is a small town in England. Is this statement true or false?

    A   True

    B   False

****

12 Shetland Islands are a part of which of these UK countries?

    A   England

    B   Wales

    C   Scotland

    D   Northern Ireland

****

13 Which of these is British Currency?

    A   Pound Sterling

    B   Dollar

    C   Riyal

    D   Yen

****

14 What is the smallest value British Pound bank note?

    A   £1

    B   £2

    C   £5

    D   £10

****

15 Which of these is the highest value British Pound bank note?

    A   £20

    B   £30

    C   £50

    D   £100

****

16   Northern Ireland and Scotland have their own banknotes, which are valid only in those countries and cannot be used in UK. Is this statement true or false?

    A   True
    B   False

****

17   Which of the following statements is correct?

    A   In Wales, many people speak Welsh, which is almost same as English with exception of few words
    B   In Wales, many people speak Welsh - a completely different language from English

****

18   What was the population of UK in 2010?

    A   4 million
    B   8 million
    C   20 million
    D   62 million

****

19   Which of the following languages is spoken by some people in Northern Ireland?

    A   Welsh
    B   Irish Gaelic
    C   Gaelic
    D   French

****

20   Which of these languages is spoken by the people in Scotland?

    A   Irish Gaelic
    B   Gaelic
    C   Irish
    D   Welsh

****

21 In recent years, the population growth has been slower, faster or same as in past?

     A   Faster

     B   No difference

     C   Slower

     D   Not known

****

22 Which TWO of these have caused increased population growth in UK?

     A   Migration into the UK

     B   Longer life expectancy

     C   Teenage Pregnancies

     D   Failed Family Planning

****

23 England constitutes almost what percent of the total population of UK?

     A   5%

     B   62%

     C   84%

     D   92%

****

24 Scotland constitutes almost what percent of the total population of UK?

     A   3%

     B   5%

     C   8%

     D   28%

****

25   What ethnic origins are included under the description 'white'?

     A   UK, Asia & Africa

     B   Europe, Australia, Canada & America

****

26   Which of the following statements is correct?

     A   Women in Britain today make up about half of the workforce

     B   Women are generally paid more than men

****

27   Which of the following statements is correct?

     A   More men than women study at university

     B   On average, girls leave school with better qualifications than boys

****

28   Over time, employment opportunities for women have increased or decreased? Mark the correct answer.

     A   Opportunities have increased

     B   Opportunities have decreased because of tougher competition

****

29   There are now lesser women in high-level positions than ever before, including senior managers. Is this statement true or false?

     A   True

     B   False

****

30   A large number of people today believe that women in Britain should stay at home and not go out to work. Is this statement true or false?

     A   True
     B   False

***

31   Women often leave work after having children. Is this statement true or false?

     A   True
     B   False

***

32   In 2009, what percent of people in UK identified themselves as Christians?

     A   70%
     B   50%
     C   15%
     D   5%

***

33   What percent of people in UK are Muslims?

     A   7.2%
     B   4.0%
     C   4.3%
     D   6.1%

***

34   What percent of people in UK are Hindus?

     A   1.1%
     B   2.5%
     C   2.0%
     D   2.1%

***

35   What percent of people in UK are Sikhs?

    A   1.0%
    B   0.3%
    C   0.8%
    D   1.7%

36   What percent of people in UK are Jews?

    A   0.3%
    B   1.7%
    C   Less than 0.5%
    D   1.2%

37   What percent of people in UK are Buddhists?

    A   0.1%
    B   0.7%
    C   Less than 0.5%
    D   0.9%

38   In 2009 citizenship survey, how many people identified themselves as having no religion?

    A   21
    B   1
    C   4
    D   2

39   Historically the United Kingdom has followed which religion?

    A   Hebrew
    B   Jewish
    C   Hindu
    D   Christian

****

40 In the UK everyone has the legal right to practise the religion of their choice. Is this statement true or false?

    A   True

    B   False

****

41 Which of these is the official Church of the state in England?

    A   Church of England

    B   Presbyterian church

    C   Roman Catholic

    D   Methodist Church

****

42 What is the Church of England called in other countries?

    A   Anglican

    B   Episcopal

    C   Methodist

    D   Baptist

****

43 What is the Church of England called in Scotland & United States?

    A   Anglican

    B   Episcopal

    C   Presbyterian

    D   Baptist

****

44 Since when has the Church of England existed?

    A   1503

    B   1534

    C   1530

    D   1504

****

45   Who is the head of the church of England?

    A   Pope
    B   Monarch
    C   Prime Minister
    D   Archbishop of Canterbury

****

46   Who is the spiritual leader of the church of England?

    A   Archbishop of Canterbury
    B   Pope
    C   Monarch
    D   Prime Minister

****

47   Who has the right to select the Archbishop?

    A   Prime Minister
    B   Church Officials
    C   Monarch
    D   Parliament

****

**48   Several Church of England bishops sit in the House of
         Lords. Is this statement true or false?**

    A   True
    B   False

****

49   Which of these is the official Church of Scotland?

    A   Baptist
    B   Presbyterian church
    C   Roman Catholic
    D   Episcopal Church

50   The Moderator is the head of the Presbyterian Church in Scotland. Is this statement true or false?

    A   True

    B   False

51   Which of these is the official Church of the state in Wales?

    A   No established Church

    B   Presbyterian church

    C   Roman Catholic Church

    D   Baptist Church

52   Which of these is the official Church of the state in Northern Ireland?

    A   No established Church

    B   Puritan Church

    C   Roman Catholic Church

    D   Methodist Church

53   Which of the following statements is correct?

    A   St Andrew is the patron saint of Scotland

    B   St George is the patron saint of Scotland

54   What is the national saint called in the UK?

    A   Holy man

    B   Archbishop

    C   Patron Saint

    D   Priest

55   Each saint has a special day. Which of the following is Saint David's day?

    A   1st March

    B   17th March

    C   23rd April

    D   30th November

****

56   Each saint has a special day. Which of the following is Saint Patrick's day?

    A   1st March

    B   17th March

    C   23rd April

    D   30th November

****

57   Each saint has a special day. Which of the following is Saint Andrew's day?

    A   1st March

    B   17th March

    C   23rd April

    D   30th November

****

58   Each saint has a special day. Which of the following is Saint George's day?

    A   1st March

    B   17th March

    C   23rd April

    D   30th November

****

59   The patron saints' days are no longer public holidays in England and Wales. Is this statement true or false?

      A   True

      B   False

*** *******

60   Which of the following statements is correct?

      A   Patron saint's days are not official holidays in Scotland and Northern Ireland

      B   Patron saint's days are official holidays in Scotland and Northern Ireland

****

61   Which of the following statements is correct?

      A   On Christmas day, people usually eat a special meal, which often includes chocolate covered eggs

      B   On Christmas day, people usually eat a special meal, which often includes roast Turkey, Christmas pudding and mince pies

****

62   Which of the following statements is correct?

      A   Very young Children believe that Santa Claus brings them presents during the night before Christmas Day

      B   Very young Children believe that Jesus Christ brings them presents during the night before Christmas Day

****

63   Which of these is Christmas Eve?

A   Evening of 25th December

B   Evening of 26th December

C   Evening of 24th December

D   Evening of 27th December

****

64   People give gifts, send cards and decorate their houses on which of these days?

A   Patron Saints' day

B   Christmas day

C   D-day

D   Remembrance day

****

65   Where do the people traditionally spend the Christmas day?

A   At home, eating a special meal with family

B   In the Church, praying and taking part in a choir

C   They spend all day in pub

D   At work

****

66   What is the day after Christmas called?

A   Boxing day

B   Christening day

C   D-day

D   Remembrance day

****

67   **When does Easter take place?**

     A   In September / October
     B   In March / April
     C   In January
     D   In June

****

68   **Which of the following statements is correct?**

     A   Easter Marks death of Jesus Christ on Good Friday and his rising from the dead on Easter Sunday
     B   Easter Marks death of Jesus Christ on Easter Sunday and his rising from the dead on Good Friday

****

69   **Which of the following statements is correct?**

     A   The day before Christmas is called Shrove Tuesday, or Pancake Day
     B   The day before Lent starts is called Shrove Tuesday, or Pancake Day

****

70   **Both Good Friday and the following Monday, called Easter Monday, are public holidays. Is this statement true or false?**

     A   True
     B   False

****

71   **Which of the following statements is correct?**

     A   Lent ends on Ash Wednesday
     B   Lent Begins on Ash Wednesday

****

72 What do people traditionally eat before fasting during 40 day lent?

  A   Chocolates
  B   Only fruit
  C   Pancakes
  D   Turkey

****

73 What do people give to each other as Easter presents, as a symbol of new life?

  A   Easter Eggs
  B   Easter Balls
  C   Easter Doughnuts
  D   Christmas lights

****

74 What does Diwali celebrate?

  A   Birth of Ram
  B   Victory of Good over Evil
  C   India's independence day
  D   Birth of Guru Nanak

****

75 What does Hannukah celebrate?

  A   It celebrates Jews' struggle for religious freedom
  B   It celebrates birth of Moses
  C   It celebrates birth of Jesus
  D   It celebrates the collapse of Soviet Union

****

76   How long does Hannukah last?

A   One day
B   One month
C   8 days
D   14 days

77   Eid al Fitr marks the end of Ramadan. Is this statement true or false?

A   True
B   False

78   Prophet Ibrahim was willing to sacrifice his son when God ordered him to. This is celebrated as which of these?

A   Hannukah
B   Eid ul Adha
C   Diwali
D   Eid Al Fitr

79   Which of the following statements is correct?

A   Many Muslims sacrifice a bird to eat during the festival of Eid ul Adha
B   Many Muslims sacrifice an animal to eat during the festival of Eid ul Adha

80   Vaisakhi (or Baisakhi) is a festival to celebrate the founding of community known as the Khalsa, by which of these?

A   Muslims
B   Roman Catholics
C   Jews
D   Sikhs

81 New Year's Eve is celebrated on the night of which of these?

    A   31st December

    B   1st January

82 Which TWO of these is true about Hogmanay?

    A   It's an Irish holiday

    B   It's a Scottish holiday

    C   It is celebrated on 31st December

    D   It is celebrated on 26th December

83 14 February, is when lovers exchange cards and gifts. What is it called?

    A   April Fools Day

    B   Halloween

    C   Valentine's day

    D   Hannukah

84 When is Mothering Sunday?

    A   The Sunday before Christmas

    B   The Sunday during Easter holidays

    C   Sunday three weeks before Easter

    D   Sunday three weeks before Christmas

85 When is Father's day?

    A   Third Sunday in June

    B   Third Sunday in January

    C   Sunday three weeks before Easter

    D   Sunday three weeks before Christmas

****

86   When is Halloween celebrated?

A   1st April
B   14th February
C   31st October
D   26th December

****

87   What does Halloween celebrate?

A   It marks victory of Good over Evil
B   It marks birth of an ancient saint
C   It is celebrated as a reminder of ghosts and witches
D   It's a pagan festival to mark the beginning of winter

****

88   Which of these is associated with Halloween?

A   Chocolate covered eggs
B   Mince Pies
C   Pumpkins
D   Jokes

****

89   On Halloween, very young people play which of these?

A   Musical chairs
B   Trick or Treat
C   Rugby
D   Board Games

****

90   When is Bonfire night celebrated?

     A   1st April

     B   14th February

     C   5th November

     D   11th November

***

91   Bonfire Night celebrates which of these?

     A   It celebrates that a group of Catholics led by Guy Fawkes failed to kill the Protestant king with a bomb in 1605

     B   It celebrates that a group of Catholics led by Guy Fawkes killed the Protestant king with a bomb in 1605

***

92   How is the Bonfire night celebrated?

     A   By wearing poppies

     B   By eating mince pies

     C   By fireworks

     D   By playing 'tick or treat'

***

93   11 November, commemorates those who died fighting for the UK and its allies. What is it called?

     A   Bonfire Night

     B   Remembrance day

     C   D day

     D   Thanksgiving day

***

94   A two minute silence at 11 am is observed on which of these days?

    A   Bonfire Night
    B   Remembrance day
    C   Thanksgiving day
    D   Christmas Day

95   Where is Wembley Stadium?

    A   London
    B   Edinburgh
    C   Cardiff
    D   Birmingham

96   How many times UK has hosted Olympic games?

    A   1
    B   2
    C   3
    D   4

97   Where was the main site for the 2012 London Olympic Games?

    A   Ilford, Greater London
    B   Hyde Park, London
    C   Wembley Stadium, London
    D   Stratford, East London

98   In 2012 Olympics, which of these positions did Britain achieve in the medals table?

    A   First
    B   Second
    C   Third
    D   Tenth

99   Which TWO of these are correct about Dr Sir Ludwig Guttmann?

  A   He is a Swiss refugee
  B   He develops new methods of treatment for spinal injuries
  C   He advices patients against taking part in exercise and sport
  D   The Paralympics have their origin in the work done by Dr Ludwig

100   Who was the first man in world to run a mile in under four minutes, in 1954?

  A   Sir Roger Bannister
  B   Bradley Wiggins
  C   Dame Ellen MacArthur
  D   Jessica Ennis

101   Which of these is a Scottish former racing driver who won the Formula 1 world championship three times?

  A   Sir Robert Watson-Watt
  B   Sir Jackie Stewart
  C   Bobby Moore
  D   Sir Bernard Lovell

102   Which of these Captained the England football team that won the World Cup in 1966?

  A   Sir Roger Bannister
  B   Sir Christopher Wren
  C   Bobby Moore
  D   Sir Ian Botham

103   Which of these won gold medals in rowing in five consecutive Olympic Games?

   A   Sir Frank Whittle
   B   Sir Jackie Stewart
   C   Sir Steve Redgrave
   D   Sir Robert Edwards

104   Which of these captained the England cricket team and holds a number of English Test cricket records ?

   A   Sir Robert Watson-Watt
   B   Sir Chris Hoy
   C   Sir Frank Whittle
   D   Sir Ian Botham

105   Which of these statements is true for Baroness Tanni Grey-Thompson?

   A   She is an athlete who uses a wheelchair and won 16 Paralympics' medals
   B   She won two gold medals for running in the 2004 Olympic Games

106   Which of these statements is true for Dame Kelly Holmes?

   A   She is the fastest person to sail around the world singlehanded
   B   She won two gold medals for running in the 2004 Olympic Games

****

107   Which TWO of these are renowned British cyclists who
       have won gold medals in Olympics?

     A   Bradley Wiggins

     B   Dame Ellen MacArthur

     C   Sir Chris Hoy

     D   David Weir

****

108   Which TWO of these are renowned Paralympians who use
       wheelchairs and have won gold medals in Paralympics?

     A   Bradley Wiggins

     B   Baroness Tanni Grey- Thompson

     C   Sir Chris Hoy

     D   David Weir

****

109   Andy Murray is the first British man to win a singles title
       in a Grand Slam tournament since 1936. Is this statement
       true or false?

     A   True

     B   False

****

110   Which of these is true about Ellie Simmonds?

     A   She won the 2012 Olympic gold medal in the
            heptathlon

     B   She is a Scottish tennis player

     C   She won gold medals for swimming at the 2008
            and 2012 Paralympics' Games

     D   She is a Scottish cyclist who has won six gold
            medals

****

111   Cricket is the UK's most popular sport. Is this statement true or false?

     A   True
     B   False

****

112   Ashes is a famous cricket competition, played between England and which of these teams?

     A   Scotland
     B   Australia
     C   France
     D   India

****

113   Which of these is UK's most popular sport?

     A   Football
     B   Cricket
     C   Golf
     D   Tennis

****

114   The first professional football clubs were formed in the late 19th century. Is this statement true or false?

     A   False
     B   True

****

115   Which of the following statements is correct?

     A   There can be great rivalry between different football clubs and among fans

     B   There cannot be any rivalry between different football clubs and among fans

****

116   Each country in the UK also has its own national team. Is this statement true or false?

     A   True

     B   False

****

117   In football, England has won how many international tournaments?

     A   10

     B   8

     C   1

     D   0

****

118   Which TWO of these originated in England?

     A   Cricket

     B   Rugby

     C   Golf

     D   Tennis

****

119   Six Nations Championship is a competition of which game?

     A   Cricket

     B   Football

     C   Golf

     D   Rugby

120   Six Nations Championship between England, Ireland, Scotland, Wales, India and Italy. Is this statement true or false?

    A   True

    B   False

121   Which TWO of these are types of rugby, with separate rules?

    A   Lawn

    B   Union

    C   Table

    D   League

122   Horse Racing has its origins in Roman times and has long association with which of these?

    A   Junkies & Gamblers

    B   Soldiers

    C   Royal family

    D   Church

123   Royal Ascot is an annual event involving which of these?

    A   Horse racing

    B   Golf

    C   Formula 1 racing

    D   Marathon

124   **Which of these is a five day event, attended by members of Royal family?**

   A   Six Nations Championship
   B   Royal Ascot
   C   Olympic Games
   D   Super League

125   **Where is the National Horse Racing museum?**

   A   Windsor
   B   Bournemouth
   C   Cornwall
   D   Suffolk

126   **The modern game of golf can be traced back to which century in Scotland?**

   A   5th century
   B   15th century
   C   18th century
   D   Early 20th Century

127   **Which of the following statements is correct?**

   A   There are very few if any golf courses in UK
   B   There are public and private golf course all over the UK

128   Which of these is known as the home of Golf?

    A   St Andrews in Scotland

    B   Cowes in Isle of Wight

    C   St Pancras in London

    D   St Albans in Hertfordshire

****

129   The Golf Open Championship is hosted by a different golf course every year. Is this statement true or false?

    A   False

    B   True

****

130   The first tennis club was founded in which of these?

    A   St Andrews in 1880

    B   Isle of Wight in 1872

    C   Leamington Spa in 1872

    D   St Albans in 1914

****

131   The Wimbledon is the oldest tennis tournament in the world. Is this statement true or false?

    A   True

    B   False

****

132   Who was the first person to sail single-handed around the world, in 1966/67?

    A   Sir Roger Bannister

    B   Sir Jackie Stewart

    C   Sir Francis Chichester

    D   Sir Robin Knox-Johnston

133   Who was the first person to sail single-handed around the world, without stopping, in 1968/69?

  A   Sir Robin Knox-Johnston
  B   Sir Jackie Stewart
  C   Sir Francis Chichester
  D   Sir Ian Botham

134   There is a popular yearly Rowing race between which of these?

  A   London & Glasgow
  B   Oxford & Cambridge Universities
  C   London & Bristol
  D   Cambridge & Edinburgh

135   What is Grand Prix?

  A   A formula 1 event
  B   A golf competition
  C   A horse race
  D   A pets exhibition

136   What is common about Damon Hill, Lewis Hamilton and Jensen Button?

  A   They play snooker together
  B   They are all Scottish
  C   They are all Formula 1 champions
  D   They were all tennis players

137   The place called Cowes on the Isle of Wight, is known for which of these?

     A   Horse racing
     B   Golf
     C   Sailing
     D   Car Racing

138   How many ski centres are there in Scotland?

     A   5
     B   10
     C   13
     D   23

139   Europe's longest dry ski slope is near which of these?

     A   Orleans, Paris
     B   Frankfurt, Germany
     C   Brussels, Belgium
     D   Edinburgh, Scotland

140   BBC organises an 8 weeks event in London since 1927, called Proms. What is it about?

     A   Car Racing
     B   Classical Music
     C   Horse Racing
     D   Quiz

141   Who was Henry Pureed (1659 - 96)?

     A   A musician/ organist
     B   A politician
     C   A poet
     D   A human right activist

142   **Sir Edward Elgar is known for which of these?**

A   Music 'The Planets'

B   Water Music

C   Music for Royal Fireworks

D   Music 'Pomp and Circumstance Marches'

143   **Which of these founded the Aldeburgh festival in Suffolk?**

A   Ralph Vaughan Williams

B   Sir William Walton

C   Benjamin Britten

D   Gustav Hoist

144   **Which TWO of these are famous music bands of 1960's?**

A   The suffragettes

B   The Beatles

C   The Rolling Stones

D   Ted & Baker

145   **Which TWO of these host musical events?**

A   Tower of London

B   The O2 in Greenwich, London

C   Scottish Exhibition and Conference Centre (SECC) in Glasgow

D   St Paul's Cathedral

146   Which of these is not a music festival?

    A   Glastonbury
    B   The Isle of Wight Festival
    C   The Grand Prix
    D   V festival

147   The National Eisteddfod is an annual cultural festival of which of these?

    A   Wales
    B   Scotland
    C   Ireland
    D   England

148   The Mercury Prize is awarded each year for best album from UK and which of these countries?

    A   Europe
    B   Ireland
    C   France
    D   United States

149   The Brit Awards is an annual event that gives awards to which TWO of these?

    A   Best British group artist
    B   Best British Solo Artist
    C   Best International solo artist
    D   Best International artist group

150   Which part of London is also known as 'Theatreland'?

A   Wembley

B   Ilford

C   Whitechapel

D   London's West End

****

151   What is Agatha Christie known for?

A   Women rights movement

B   Politics

C   Murder Mystery Drama Writing

D   Ice dancing

****

152   Which of these is an example of operas?

A   The Pirates of Penzance

B   Pirates of the Caribbean

C   Harry Potter and the Deathly Halos

D   Charlie & The Chocolate Factory

****

153   Light-hearted plays based on fairy stories, are produced around Christmas time. What are these called?

A   Proms

B   Pantomimes

C   Phantoms

D   Operas

****

154   Where does Edinburgh festival take place?

     A   London

     B   Glasgow

     C   Edinburgh

     D   Leicester

155   The Fringe' (Festival) in Edinburgh, mainly consists of which of these?

     A   Flowers exhibition

     B   Property Exhibition

     C   Painting & Photography

     D   Theatre and comedy performances

156   The Laurence Olivier Awards take place annually for which of these categories?

     A   Best Formula 1 driver

     B   Best Football player

     C   Best director, best actor & best actress

     D   Best Athlete

157   Art from the middle ages mostly had a religious theme. It was lost after which of these?

     A   Protestant Reformation

     B   First World war

     C   2nd World War

     D   War of Roses

158   Which TWO of these were portrait painters?

    A   Baroness Tanni Grey-Thompson

    B   David Allan

    C   Dame Ellen MacArthur

    D   Thomas Gainsborough

159   Which TWO of these were landscape painters?

    A   Joseph Turner

    B   John Constable

    C   Sir John Lavery

    D   Dame Ellen MacArthur

160   Who were Pre-Raphaelites?

    A   A football team

    B   Pop Music Band

    C   A group of Artists

    D   Bishops

161   Which of these is a Walsh artist best known for his engravings and stained glass?

    A   John Petts

    B   Lucian Freud

    C   David Hockney

    D   Sir John Lavery

162   The Turner Prize is recognised as one of the most prestigious visual art awards in Europe, and celebrates which of these?

    A   Contemporary art

    B   Ice Dancing

    C   Pop Music

    D   Acting

****

163   Great Cathedrals and Churches, like the ones in Durham & Lincoln, were built in which of these times?

   A   Stone Age
   B   Iron Age
   C   Middle Ages
   D   World War I

****

164   In the 17th century, Inigo Jones took inspiration from classical architecture to design which of these?

   A   Tower of London
   B   The Big Ben
   C   The Queen's House at Greenwich
   D   St Paul's Cathedral

****

165   Which of these designed the new St Pauls Cathedral?

   A   Dame Zaha Hadid
   B   Sir Christopher Wren
   C   Sir Terence Conran
   D   Alexander McQueen

****

166   In the 19th century, the medieval 'gothic' style architecture became popular again. Which TWO of these buildings are examples?

   A   Houses of Parliament, London
   B   Excel London
   C   St Pancras station
   D   Wembley Stadium

****

167 Which of these designed New Delhi to be the seat of government in India?

  A   Dame Zaha Hadid

  B   Sir Christopher Wren

  C   Sir Terence Conran

  D   Sir Edwin Lutyens

168 Which of these is an annual flower show showcasing garden designs from Britain and around the world?

  A   Wembley Flower Show

  B   Chelsea Flower Show

  C   Glastonbury Flower Festival

  D   Edinburgh Festival

169 Which of the following statements is correct?

  A   Vivienne Westwood is a 20th century interior designer

  B   Sir Terence Conran is a 20th century interior designer

170 Which of the following statements is correct?

  A   Alexander McQueen is a leading fashion designer

  B   Dame Zaha Hadid is a leading fashion designer

171 Which British author introduced the character of James Bond?

  A   Agatha Christie

  B   Arthur Conan Doyle

  C   Ian Fleming

  D   Jim Thompson

****

172 In 2003, which novel by JRR Tolkien was voted the country's best- loved novel?

    A   The Lord of the Rings

    B   The Pirates of the Caribbean

    C   The Witches of Oz

    D   Harry Potter & the Deathly Hallows

****

173 The Man Booker Prize for Fiction is awarded annually for the best fiction novel written by an author from which of these countries?

    A   The Commonwealth, Ireland & Zimbabwe

    B   Ireland

    C   Zimbabwe

    D   UK & Ireland

****

174 What was the name of the English novelist who wrote 'Pride & Prejudice' and 'Sense & Sensibility'?

    A   Henry Purcell

    B   Charles Dickens

    C   Jane Austen

    D   Sir John Lavery

****

175 Which of these is a renowned novelist?

    A   Charles Dickens

    B   Sir William Walton

    C   Mo Farah

    D   Andy Murray

****

176   Which of these is not a novelist?

    A   JK Rowling
    B   Charles Dickens
    C   Sir Arthur Conan Doyle
    D   Dame Kelly Holmes

****

177   Who created the fictional character Sherlock Holmes?

    A   Shakespeare
    B   Charles Dickens
    C   Sir Arthur Conan Doyle
    D   Roald Dahl

****

178   Who is the writer of famous series for children 'The Harry Potter'?

    A   Jane Austen
    B   Evelyn Waugh
    C   JK Rowling
    D   Dame Kelly Holmes

****

179   Which of these introduced the characters such as Scrooge (a mean person) and Mr Micawber (always hopeful)?

    A   Agatha Christie
    B   Arthur Conan Doyle
    C   William Shakespeare
    D   Charles Dickens

****

180   Which of these is not a translated poem from the middle ages?

    A   The Green Knight
    B   The Black Knight
    C   Sir Gawain
    D   Canterbury Tales

****

181   Paradise lost is a poem inspired by religious views by which of these poets?

    A   John Milton
    B   Charles Dickens
    C   Shakespeare
    D   William Wordsworth

****

182   As well as plays, Shakespeare wrote many poems. Is this statement true or false?

    A   True
    B   False

****

183   Sir Walter Scott wrote poems and novels inspired by which of these?

    A   England
    B   Ireland
    C   France
    D   Scotland

****

184   Writings of which TWO of these are known to be influenced by religious beliefs?

     A   Graham Greene

     B   William Wordsworth

     C   John Milton

     D   Sir Walter Scott

****

185   Who amongst these is not a famous 19th century poet?

     A   William Blake

     B   John Keats

     C   Charles Dickens

     D   Elizabeth Browning

****

186   Wilfred Owen and Siegfried Sassoon - were inspired to write poems about their experiences of which of these?

     A   First World War

     B   Poverty

     C   Religion

     D   Royal Coronations

****

187   Some of the best-known poets are buried or commemorated in which part in Westminster Abbey?

     A   Leaders Corner

     B   Art Square

     C   Poets' Corner

     D   Corner of peace

****

188   Whose famous poem is this 'I wandered lonely as a cloud'?

    A   William Blake

    B   John Keats

    C   Shakespeare

    D   William Wordsworth

****

189   In UK, a lot of people have gardens at home and spend their free time looking after them. Is this statement true or false?

    A   True

    B   False

****

190   Some people rent additional land for gardening to grow fruit & vegetables. What is it called?

    A   The vege spot

    B   The allotment

    C   The green

    D   The patch

****

191   Which TWO of these are famous gardens in UK?

    A   Kew Gardens

    B   Sissinghurst

    C   Gardens of Peace

    D   Carnarvon Castle

****

192   All countries of UK have flowers particularly associated
        with them. Which of the flower represents England?

        A   The Rose
        B   The Thistle
        C   The Daffodil
        D   The Shamrock

****

193   All countries of UK have flowers particularly associated
        with them. Which of the flower represents Northern
        Ireland?

        A   The Rose
        B   The Thistle
        C   The Daffodil
        D   The Shamrock

****

194   All countries of UK have flowers particularly associated
        with them. Which of the flower represents Wales?

        A   The Rose
        B   The Thistle
        C   The Daffodil
        D   The Shamrock

****

195   All countries of UK have flowers particularly associated
        with them. Which of the flower represents Scotland?

        A   The Rose
        B   The Thistle
        C   The Daffodil
        D   The Shamrock

****

196   Most towns and cities have a central shopping area, called which of these?

    A   Centre Point

    B   Shopping point

    C   Town Centre

    D   Junction

197   Most shops in the UK are open for how many days a week?

    A   3

    B   5

    C   7

    D   8

198   Most shops open for longer during Sundays and public holidays. Is this statement true or false?

    A   True

    B   False

199   Fish & Chips are traditional Welsh food. Is this statement true or false?

    A   True

    B   False

200   Which TWO of these are traditional foods in England?

    A   Spicy Curry

    B   Rice Pilau

    C   Roast Beef

    D   Yorkshire Puddings

201 Haggis - a sheep's stomach stuffed with offal suet, onions and oatmeal, is a traditional food of which area of UK?

  A England
  B Ireland
  C Scotland
  D Wales

202 Ulster Fry is a traditional food of which area of UK?

  A England
  B Northern Ireland
  C Scotland
  D Wales

203 Films were first shown publicly in the UK in which year?

  A 1896
  B 1996
  C 1755
  D 1914

204 From the early days of the cinema, British actors have worked in both the UK and which of these countries?

  A India
  B USA
  C France
  D Ireland

205   Which of these characters became famous in silent
       movies for his tramp character ?

    A   James Bond
    B   Mr Beans
    C   Sherlock Holmes
    D   Charlie Chaplin

206   Who was Sir Alfred Hitchcock?

    A   Actor who played Sherlock Holmes
    B   Creator of character of Mr Beans
    C   A famous writer
    D   A famous film director

207   Which of these is not a British film director?

    A   Sir Alfred Hitchcock
    B   Ridley Scott
    C   Dame Ellen MacArthur
    D   Sir David Lean

208   Which of these studios has a claim to being the oldest
       continuously working film studio facility in the world?

    A   Fox Studios
    B   Ealing
    C   Hollywood
    D   Disney

209   In film industry, what did Nick Park win Oscars for?

    A   Animated films
    B   Music
    C   Dialogue writing
    D   Acting

210   Which TWO of these are Oscar winning British actors?

    A   Colin Firth

    B   Dame Judy Dench

    C   Nick Clegg

    D   George Osborne

211   The British Academy Film Awards, by British Academy of Film and Television Arts (BAFTA), are equivalent of which of these?

    A   Nobel Prize

    B   Grammy awards

    C   Oscars

    D   Lux Style Awards

212   British film 'The 39 Steps' (1935) was directed by which of these?

    A   David Lean

    B   Carol Reed

    C   Ken Russell

    D   Alfred Hitchcock

213   British film 'The Third Man' (1949) was directed by which of these?

    A   David Lean

    B   Carol Reed

    C   Ken Russell

    D   Alfred Hitchcock

214   British film 'Women in Love' (1969) was directed by which
        of these?

        A   Ken Russell
        B   Mike Newell
        C   Nicolas Roeg
        D   Nicolas Roeg

215   British film 'Lawrence of Arabia' (1962) was directed by
        which of these?

        A   Ken Russell
        B   Carol Reed
        C   David Lean
        D   Alfred Hitchcock

216   British film 'Don't Look Now' (1973) was directed by
        which of these?

        A   David Lean
        B   Carol Reed
        C   Ken Russell
        D   Nicolas Roeg

217   Which TWO of these films were directed by British
        Director David Lean?

        A   Brief Encounter (1945)
        B   The Third Man (1949)
        C   Lawrence of Arabia (1962)
        D   The Belles of St Trinian's (1954)

218   British film 'Four Weddings and a Funeral' (1994) was directed by which of these?

    A   Mike Newell
    B   Carol Reed
    C   Ken Russell
    D   Nicolas Roeg

****

219   Cartoons attacking prominent politicians and sometimes Royal family, became popular in which century?

    A   17th
    B   18th
    C   19th
    D   20th

****

220   Before TV, which of these form of variety theatre was very common in UK?

    A   Music Hall
    B   Comic theatre
    C   Funland
    D   Comic circus

****

221   In UK, some TV channels are free to watch and others require a paid subscription. Is this statement true or false?

    A   True
    B   False

****

222   Which TWO of these are names of popular regular soap operas?

    A   Antiques Road Show

    B   East Enders

    C   Coronation Street

    D   Prime Minister Questions

223   In UK, only people who watch television on a TV set are required to have a TV licence. Is this statement true or false?

    A   True

    B   False

224   If you have more than one equipment to watch TV at home, how many licences you will need?

    A   One only, as it covers all of the equipment in one home

    B   One per equipment, so you will need more than one licence

    C   You do not need a licence

    D   It depends on how many rooms you have in the house

225   In a shared house where people are renting different rooms under separate tenancy agreements, how many TV licences will be required?

    A   Each tenant will require a separate licence to watch his/ her own TV on any equipment

    B   Only one licence by the landlord will be enough to cover all the tenants

    C   You do not need a licence

    D   It depends on how many rooms you have in the house

226   Who can apply for a free TV licence?

A   Pregnant women

B   Children under 18 years

C   People over 75

D   Blind People

227   Who can apply for a 50% discount for a TV licence?

A   Pregnant women

B   Children under 18 years

C   People over 76

D   Blind People

228   You will receive a fine of up to what amount if you watch TV but do not have a TV licence?

A   £50

B   £80

C   £100

D   £1,000

229   Where does the money from the TV licences go?

A   BBC

B   Sky News

C   Inland Revenue

D   British Film Industry

230   Which TWO of these are true about BBC?

A   BBC is the largest broadcaster in the world

B   Wholly Private

C   Independent of government

D   US Based

231   UK channels, other than BBC, are funded by which of these?

    A   BBC

    B   Subscriptions & Advertisements

    C   Inland Revenue

    D   Royal Family

232   Like television BBC radio stations are funded by TV licences. Is this statement true or false?

    A   True

    B   False

233   The popular 'Facebook' & 'Twitter' are names of which of these?

    A   Popular Novels

    B   Popular Books from 19th century

    C   Music Bands

    D   Social Networking Websites

234   Which TWO of these are traditional pub games?

    A   Pool

    B   Darts

    C   Football

    D   Cricket

235   What is the minimum age to buy alcohol in a pub?

    A   21

    B   16

    C   18

    D   No age bar

236 When they are 14, people can drink wine or beer with a meal in a pub as long as they are with someone over 18. Is this statement true or false?

    A   True
    B   False

237 Night clubs with dancing and music usually open and close earlier or later than pubs?

    A   Later than pubs
    B   Earlier than pubs

238 What is the minimum age to go to betting shops or gambling clubs?

    A   21
    B   16
    C   18
    D   No age bar

239 What is the minimum age to buy a lottery ticket or a scratch card?

    A   14
    B   16
    C   18
    D   21

240 Why do people keep pets like cats or dogs? Mark TWO correct answers.

    A   For Company
    B   To look after them
    C   For Security
    D   For show off

****

241   Who is responsible for keeping the dog under control and for cleaning up after the animal in a public place?

A   Council
B   Neighbour
C   Owner
D   Nobody

****

242   Which animal must wear a collar showing the name and address of the owner in public places?

A   Dog
B   Cat
C   Goldfish
D   Parrot

****

243   From where are the Vaccinations and medical treatment for animals available?

A   Veterinary Surgeons
B   NHS
C   NSPCC
D   Oxfam

****

244   How many national parks are there in England, Wales and Scotland?

A   100
B   60
C   40
D   15

****

245   Famous landmarks exist in towns, cities and the countryside throughout the UK, and public is not allowed to see them. Is this statement true or false?

    A   True
    B   False

****

246   The National Trust was founded in 1895, by which of these?

    A   The National Geographic Channel
    B   Government
    C   Volunteers
    D   BBC

****

247   How many volunteers are there to keep the National Trust running?

    A   100
    B   3100
    C   10000
    D   61000

****

248   Which of these is a famous UK landmark?

    A   Big Ben
    B   Eifel Tower
    C   Tower of Liberty
    D   Taj Mahal

****

249   When was the clock tower named 'Elizabeth Tower' in honour of Queen Elizabeth II?

    A   At her coronation

    B   On birth of Prince Charles, her heir to the throne

    C   On her Diamond Jubilee

    D   It was never named Elizabeth tower

****

250   Eden project in Cornwall, involves which of these?

    A   Giant Greenhouses

    B   Collection of Modern Arts

    C   Collection of Music archives

    D   Picture Gallery

****

251   Edinburgh Castle's long history dates back to what times?

    A   Stone Age

    B   Bronze age

    C   Iron Age

    D   Middle Ages

****

252   How old is the Giant's Causeway in Northern Ireland?

    A   1000 years old

    B   1400 years old

    C   10,000 years old

    D   50,000 years old

****

253   What is the Giant's Causeway in Northern Ireland made of?

    A   Sand

    B   Lava

    C   Fossils

    D   Wood

254 Which one of these is the largest expanse of fresh water in mainland Britain?

    A   Loch ness Monster

    B   Loch Fyne

    C   Loch Lomond

    D   River Thames

255 When was London Eye built?

    A   Start of New Millennium

    B   Start of 2012 Olympics

    C   After World War 1

    D   After World War 2

256 Where is London Eye?

    A   In Nottingham

    B   In Londonderry

    C   In London

    D   In Edinburgh

257 Where is Snowdonia?

    A   Wales

    B   Scotland

    C   Cornwall

    D   Northern Ireland

258 The Tower of London was first built by which of these kings?

    A   King James II

    B   William the Conqueror

    C   King John

    D   King Charles II

****

259   Tours of the Tower of London are given by which of these?

     A   Police officers

     B   Soldiers

     C   Beefeaters

     D   Anybody

****

260   Where can general public see the Crown jewels?

     A   Buckingham Palace

     B   House of Lords

     C   Tower of London

     D   Windsor Palace

****

261   Which of these is the largest National Park in the UK?

     A   Peak District

     B   Inverness

     C   Snowdonia

     D   Lake District

****

262   Which of these is the biggest stretch of water in Lake District?

     A   Grasmere

     B   Windermere

     C   Derwent Water

     D   Buttermere

****

ANSWER KEY

Q.#	Answer	Reference	
		Chapter	Page No.
1.	D	A modern, thriving society	p. 71
2.	C	A modern, thriving society	p. 71
3.	A	A modern, thriving society	p. 72
4.	C	A modern, thriving society	p. 72
5.	D	A modern, thriving society	p. 72
6.	A	A modern, thriving society	p. 72
7.	B & D	A modern, thriving society	p. 72
8.	A & D	A modern, thriving society	p. 72
9.	C	A modern, thriving society	p. 72
10.	B & D	A modern, thriving society	p. 72
11.	B	A modern, thriving society	p. 72
12.	C	A modern, thriving society	p. 72
13.	A	A modern, thriving society	p. 74
14.	C	A modern, thriving society	p. 74
15.	C	A modern, thriving society	p. 74
16.	B	A modern, thriving society	p. 74
17.	B	A modern, thriving society	p. 74
18.	D	A modern, thriving society	p. 74
19.	B	A modern, thriving society	p. 74
20.	B	A modern, thriving society	p. 74
21.	A	A modern, thriving society	p. 75
22.	A & B	A modern, thriving society	p. 75

ANSWER KEY

Q.#	Answer	Reference	
		Chapter	Page No.
23.	C	A modern, thriving society	p. 75
24.	C	A modern, thriving society	p. 76
25.	B	A modern, thriving society	p. 75
26.	A	A modern, thriving society	p. 75
27.	B	A modern, thriving society	p. 75
28.	A	A modern, thriving society	p. 76
29.	B	A modern, thriving society	p. 76
30.	B	A modern, thriving society	p. 76
31.	B	A modern, thriving society	p. 76
32.	A	A modern, thriving society	p. 76
33.	B	A modern, thriving society	p. 76
34.	C	A modern, thriving society	p. 76
35.	A	A modern, thriving society	p. 76
36.	C	A modern, thriving society	p. 76
37.	C	A modern, thriving society	p. 76
38.	A	A modern, thriving society	p. 76
39.	D	A modern, thriving society	p. 76
40.	A	A modern, thriving society	p. 76
41.	A	A modern, thriving society	p. 77
42.	A	A modern, thriving society	p. 77
43.	B	A modern, thriving society	p. 77
44.	C	A modern, thriving society	p. 77

ANSWER KEY

Q.#	Answer	Reference	
		Chapter	Page No.
45.	B	A modern, thriving society	p. 77
46.	A	A modern, thriving society	p. 77
47.	C	A modern, thriving society	p. 77
48.	A	A modern, thriving society	p. 77
49.	B	A modern, thriving society	p. 77
50.	A	A modern, thriving society	p. 77
51.	A	A modern, thriving society	p. 77
52.	A	A modern, thriving society	p. 77
53.	A	A modern, thriving society	p. 77
54.	C	A modern, thriving society	p. 77
55.	A	A modern, thriving society	p. 77
56.	B	A modern, thriving society	p. 77
57.	D	A modern, thriving society	p. 77
58.	C	A modern, thriving society	p. 77
59.	A	A modern, thriving society	p. 78
60.	B	A modern, thriving society	p. 78
61.	B	A modern, thriving society	p. 79
62.	A	A modern, thriving society	p. 79
63.	C	A modern, thriving society	p. 79
64.	B	A modern, thriving society	p. 79
65.	A	A modern, thriving society	p. 79
66.	A	A modern, thriving society	p. 80

ANSWER KEY

Q.#	Answer	Reference	
		Chapter	Page No.
67.	B	A modern, thriving society	p. 80
68.	A	A modern, thriving society	p. 80
69.	B	A modern, thriving society	p. 80
70.	A	A modern, thriving society	p. 80
71.	B	A modern, thriving society	p. 80
72.	C	A modern, thriving society	p. 80
73.	A	A modern, thriving society	p. 80
74.	B	A modern, thriving society	p. 81
75.	A	A modern, thriving society	p. 81
76.	C	A modern, thriving society	p. 81
77.	A	A modern, thriving society	p. 82
78.	B	A modern, thriving society	p. 82
79.	B	A modern, thriving society	p. 82
80.	D	A modern, thriving society	p. 82
81.	A	A modern, thriving society	p. 82
82.	B & C	A modern, thriving society	p. 82
83.	C	A modern, thriving society	p. 82
84.	C	A modern, thriving society	p. 82
85.	A	A modern, thriving society	p. 82
86.	C	A modern, thriving society	p. 82
87.	D	A modern, thriving society	p. 82
88.	C	A modern, thriving society	p. 82

ANSWER KEY

Q.#	Answer	Reference	
		Chapter	Page No.
89.	B	A modern, thriving society	p. 82
90.	C	A modern, thriving society	p. 83
91.	A	A modern, thriving society	p. 83
92.	C	A modern, thriving society	p. 83
93.	B	A modern, thriving society	p. 83
94.	B	A modern, thriving society	p. 83
95.	A	A modern, thriving society	p. 84
96.	C	A modern, thriving society	p. 84
97.	D	A modern, thriving society	p. 84
98.	C	A modern, thriving society	p. 84
99.	B & D	A modern, thriving society	p. 84-85
100.	A	A modern, thriving society	p. 85
101.	B	A modern, thriving society	p. 85
102.	C	A modern, thriving society	p. 85
103.	C	A modern, thriving society	p. 85
104.	D	A modern, thriving society	p. 85
105.	A	A modern, thriving society	p. 85
106.	B	A modern, thriving society	p. 85
107.	A & C	A modern, thriving society	p. 85
108.	B & D	A modern, thriving society	p. 85
109.	A	A modern, thriving society	p. 85
110.	C	A modern, thriving society	p. 85

ANSWER KEY

Q.#	Answer	Reference	
		Chapter	Page No.
111.	B	A modern, thriving society	p. 86
112.	B	A modern, thriving society	p. 87
113.	A	A modern, thriving society	p. 87
114.	B	A modern, thriving society	p. 87
115.	A	A modern, thriving society	p. 87
116.	A	A modern, thriving society	p. 87
117.	C	A modern, thriving society	p. 88
118.	A & B	A modern, thriving society	p. 86 -87
119.	D	A modern, thriving society	p. 88
120.	B	A modern, thriving society	p. 88
121.	B & D	A modern, thriving society	p. 88
122.	C	A modern, thriving society	p. 88
123.	A	A modern, thriving society	p. 88
124.	B	A modern, thriving society	p. 88
125.	D	A modern, thriving society	p. 88
126.	B	A modern, thriving society	p. 88
127.	B	A modern, thriving society	p. 88
128.	A	A modern, thriving society	p. 88
129.	B	A modern, thriving society	p. 89
130.	C	A modern, thriving society	p. 89
131.	A	A modern, thriving society	p. 89
132.	C	A modern, thriving society	p. 89

ANSWER KEY

Q.#	Answer	Reference	
		Chapter	Page No.
133.	A	A modern, thriving society	p. 89
134.	B	A modern, thriving society	p. 89
135.	A	A modern, thriving society	p. 89
136.	C	A modern, thriving society	p. 89
137.	C	A modern, thriving society	p. 89
138.	A	A modern, thriving society	p. 89
139.	D	A modern, thriving society	p. 89
140.	B	A modern, thriving society	p. 90
141.	A	A modern, thriving society	p. 90
142.	D	A modern, thriving society	p. 90
143.	C	A modern, thriving society	p. 91
144.	B & C	A modern, thriving society	p. 92
145.	B & C	A modern, thriving society	p. 92
146.	C	A modern, thriving society	p. 92
147.	A	A modern, thriving society	p. 92
148.	B	A modern, thriving society	p. 92
149.	A & B	A modern, thriving society	p. 92
150.	D	A modern, thriving society	p. 93
151.	C	A modern, thriving society	p. 93
152.	A	A modern, thriving society	p. 93
153.	B	A modern, thriving society	p. 93
154.	C	A modern, thriving society	p. 93

ANSWER KEY

Q.#	Answer	Reference	
		Chapter	Page No.
155.	D	A modern, thriving society	p. 93
156.	C	A modern, thriving society	p. 93
157.	A	A modern, thriving society	p. 93
158.	B & D	A modern, thriving society	p. 94
159.	A & B	A modern, thriving society	p. 94
160.	C	A modern, thriving society	p. 94
161.	A	A modern, thriving society	p. 95
162.	A	A modern, thriving society	p. 95
163.	C	A modern, thriving society	p. 96
164.	C	A modern, thriving society	p. 96
165.	B	A modern, thriving society	p. 96
166.	A & C	A modern, thriving society	p. 96
167.	D	A modern, thriving society	p. 96
168.	B	A modern, thriving society	p. 97
169.	B	A modern, thriving society	p. 97
170.	A	A modern, thriving society	p. 97
171.	C	A modern, thriving society	p. 97
172.	A	A modern, thriving society	p. 97
173.	A	A modern, thriving society	p. 97
174.	C	A modern, thriving society	p. 98
175.	A	A modern, thriving society	p. 98
176.	D	A modern, thriving society	p. 98

ANSWER KEY

Q.#	Answer	Reference	
		Chapter	Page No.
177.	C	A modern, thriving society	p. 98
178.	C	A modern, thriving society	p. 98
179.	D	A modern, thriving society	p. 98
180.	B	A modern, thriving society	p. 99
181.	A	A modern, thriving society	p. 99
182.	A	A modern, thriving society	p. 99
183.	D	A modern, thriving society	p. 99
184.	A & C	A modern, thriving society	p. 99
185.	C	A modern, thriving society	p. 99
186.	A	A modern, thriving society	p. 99
187.	C	A modern, thriving society	p. 99
188.	D	A modern, thriving society	p. 99
189.	A	A modern, thriving society	p. 101
190.	B	A modern, thriving society	p. 101
191.	A & B	A modern, thriving society	p. 101
192.	A	A modern, thriving society	p. 101
193.	D	A modern, thriving society	p. 101
194.	C	A modern, thriving society	p. 101
195.	B	A modern, thriving society	p. 101
196.	C	A modern, thriving society	p. 102
197.	C	A modern, thriving society	p. 102
198.	B	A modern, thriving society	p. 102

ANSWER KEY

Q.#	Answer	Reference	
		Chapter	Page No.
199.	B	A modern, thriving society	p. 102
200.	C & D	A modern, thriving society	p. 102
201.	C	A modern, thriving society	p. 102
202.	B	A modern, thriving society	p. 102
203.	A	A modern, thriving society	p. 103
204.	B	A modern, thriving society	p. 103
205.	D	A modern, thriving society	p. 103
206.	D	A modern, thriving society	p. 103
207.	C	A modern, thriving society	p. 103
208.	B	A modern, thriving society	p. 103
209.	A	A modern, thriving society	p. 103
210.	A & B	A modern, thriving society	p. 103
211.	C	A modern, thriving society	p. 103
212.	D	A modern, thriving society	p. 104
213.	B	A modern, thriving society	p. 104
214.	A	A modern, thriving society	p. 104
215.	C	A modern, thriving society	p. 104
216.	D	A modern, thriving society	p. 104
217.	A & C	A modern, thriving society	p. 104
218.	A	A modern, thriving society	p. 104
219.	B	A modern, thriving society	p. 104
220.	A	A modern, thriving society	p. 105

ANSWER KEY

Q.#	Answer	Reference	
		Chapter	Page No.
221.	A	A modern, thriving society	p. 105
222.	C & B	A modern, thriving society	p. 105
223.	B	A modern, thriving society	p. 105
224.	A	A modern, thriving society	p. 105
225.	A	A modern, thriving society	p. 105
226.	C	A modern, thriving society	p. 105
227.	D	A modern, thriving society	p. 105
228.	D	A modern, thriving society	p. 105
229.	A	A modern, thriving society	p. 105
230.	A & C	A modern, thriving society	p. 106
231.	B	A modern, thriving society	p. 106
232.	A	A modern, thriving society	p. 106
233.	D	A modern, thriving society	p. 106
234.	A & B	A modern, thriving society	p. 106
235.	C	A modern, thriving society	p. 106
236.	B	A modern, thriving society	p. 106
237.	A	A modern, thriving society	p. 106
238.	C	A modern, thriving society	p. 106
239.	B	A modern, thriving society	p. 107
240.	A & B	A modern, thriving society	p. 107
241.	C	A modern, thriving society	p. 107
242.	A	A modern, thriving society	p. 107

ANSWER KEY

Q.#	Answer	Reference	
		Chapter	Page No.
243.	A	A modern, thriving society	p. 107
244.	D	A modern, thriving society	p. 107
245.	B	A modern, thriving society	p. 107
246.	C	A modern, thriving society	p. 107
247.	D	A modern, thriving society	p. 107
248.	A	A modern, thriving society	p. 108
249.	C	A modern, thriving society	p. 108
250.	A	A modern, thriving society	p. 109
251.	D	A modern, thriving society	p. 110
252.	D	A modern, thriving society	p. 110
253.	B	A modern, thriving society	p. 111
254.	C	A modern, thriving society	p. 112
255.	A	A modern, thriving society	p. 113
256.	C	A modern, thriving society	p. 113
257.	A	A modern, thriving society	p. 114
258.	B	A modern, thriving society	p. 115
259.	C	A modern, thriving society	p. 115
260.	C	A modern, thriving society	p. 115
261.	D	A modern, thriving society	p. 116
262.	B	A modern, thriving society	p. 116

Chapter 5:

The UK Government, the Law & Your Role

1   **What is the system of government in the UK?**

        A   Presidential democracy

        B   Direct democracy

        C   Parliamentary democracy

        D   Federal

****

2   **Democracy is a system of government in which, which of these applies?**

        A   Whole population gets a say

        B   Whole male population gets a say

        C   Whole adult population gets a say

        D   Only highly educated people get a say

****

3   **Who were eligible to vote at the turn of 19th century?**

        A   All adult men & women

        B   All adult men

        C   Men over 21 years of age and who owned a certain amount of property

        D   Only Nobles & Royals

****

4   **When did political parties began to involve ordinary men and women as members?**

        A   17th century

        B   18th century

        C   19th century

        D   20th century

****

5   In 1830s and 1840s, the Chartists campaigned for reform. They wanted six changes. Which TWO of these were their demands?

      A   Elections every year

      B   Voting right for every man

      C   Slaves to be freed

      D   Open Ballots

****

6   Most of the reforms demanded by the Chartists had been adopted by which year?

      A   1918

      B   1928

      C   1947

      D   1850

****

7   In 1969, the voting age was reduced from 21 to the current age of which one of these?

      A   14

      B   20

      C   16

      D   18

****

8   British constitution is written down in a single document like other countries. Is this statement true or false?

      A   True

      B   False

****

9   Which of the following statements is correct?

   A   Some people believe that constitution should
          remain unwritten as it allows more flexibility and
          better government
   B   Some people believe that constitution should
          remain unwritten so that laws can be broken easily

****

10   UK had several revolutions which led permanently to
       totally new systems of government. Is this statement true
       or false?

   A   True
   B   False

****

11   Which of the following statements is correct?

   A   The UK has a constitutional monarchy
   B   The UK does not have a constitutional monarchy

****

12   Which of these are parts of government in UK? Mark TWO
       correct answers.

   A   The Banks
   B   The Prime Minister & Monarch
   C   The Judiciary & Police
   D   The Press

****

13 **Who is the head of state of the United Kingdom?**

    A   Queen Elizabeth I

    B   Queen Elizabeth II

    C   King George II

    D   Prince Philip

***

14 **In Constitutional Monarchy, who rules the country?**

    A   The Prime Minister

    B   The Monarch

***

15 **Queen can make decisions for the government. Is this statement true or false?**

    A   True

    B   False

***

16 **Since when has Queen Elizabeth II reigned?**

    A   1945

    B   1950

    C   1952

    D   1955

***

17 **Who is the Queen married to?**

    A   Prince William

    B   Prince Harry

    C   Prince Philip

    D   King James

****

18   What was the big event relating to the Queen in 2012?

    A   Her 60th Birthday

    B   Her 60 years of reign - Diamond Jubilee

    C   She was given the Nobel peace prize

    D   She was on a world tour

****

19   Who is the heir to the throne?

    A   Prince William

    B   Prince Harry

    C   Prince Philip

    D   Prince Charles

****

20   What roles does the Queen have in government? Select TWO answers.

    A   Keeping order during political debates

    B   Important ceremonial roles

    C   Parliamentary roles

    D   Making sure rules are followed

****

21   Who opens the new Parliamentary session each year?

    A   The Pope

    B   The Queen

    C   The Prime Minister

    D   House of Lords

****

22   The Queen receives foreign ambassadors and high commissioners & entertains visiting heads of state. Is this statement true or false?

    A   True
    B   False

****

23   What is the National Anthem of UK?

    A   God save us
    B   God save the king
    C   God save the Queen
    D   God save the princes

****

24   When do new residents have to swear or affirm allegiance to the Queen?

    A   When applying for life in the UK test
    B   When applying for visa
    C   When applying for passport
    D   In the citizenship ceremony

****

25   Voters in each constituency elect their member of Parliament [MP] in which elections?

    A   General
    B   Local
    C   International
    D   European

****

26   The elected MPs (members of parliament) make which house of Parliament?

     A   House of Lords

     B   House of Commons

     C   Royal House

     D   Ordinary House

****

27   Most of the members of parliament are independent and not from a political party. Is this true or false?

     A   True

     B   False

****

28   After elections, who forms the government?

     A   Political Party with majority MPs forms the government

     B   Political Party with most influential nobles forms the government

     C   Political party with most experienced politicians forms the government

     D   Political Party favourite to the Queen forms the government

****

29   Who forms the government if no party gets a majority?

     A   The Queen rules if no party wins majority

     B   The previous government continues if no party won majority in new elections

     C   There are always re-elections if no party wins majority

     D   Two parties can join to make a coalition government if no party wins the majority

****

30   The Houses of Parliament in London, are a world heritage
        site. Is this statement true or false?

        A   True
        B   False

****

31   Which is regarded as the more important of the two
        chambers in Parliament?

        A   House of Lords
        B   House of Commons
        C   House of General Public
        D   House of Queen

****

32   The prime minister and all the members of the cabinet
        are members of the House of Lords. Is this statement true
        or false?

        A   True
        B   False

****

33   Which of the following each MP represent?

        A   A city
        B   A town
        C   A constituency
        D   A county

****

34   **Which TWO of these are responsibilities of an MP?**

  A   Represent everyone in their constituency
  B   Scrutinise and comment on what the government is doing
  C   Weekly meetings with people in their area
  D   Providing free private medical care to voters

****

35   **Members of the House of Lords, known as peers, are elected by the public. Is this statement true or false?**

  A   True
  B   False

****

36   **Until 1958 all peers [members of House of Lords] belonged to which TWO of these groups?**

  A   Prominent Celebrities from Show Business
  B   Hereditary, means they inherited their title
  C   Senior Judges & Bishops
  D   Temporary

****

37   **Since 1958, the prime minister has had the power to nominate peers just for their own lifetime. What are these called?**

  A   Life Peers
  B   Live Peers
  C   Temporary Peers
  D   Transient Peers

****

38   Which TWO of these can nominate Peers?

       A   Prime Minister

       B   Leader of Opposition party

       C   Police

       D   Public

****

39   All the hereditary peers have an automatic right to attend the House of Lords unrestricted. Is this statement true or false?

       A   True

       B   False

****

40   Which house of parliament is normally more independent of the government?

       A   House of Lords

       B   House of Commons

****

41   House of Lords can do which TWO of these?

       A   Can overrule laws made by House of Commons

       B   Propose new laws

       C   Check the laws passed by House of Commons to ensure they are fit for purpose

       D   Can overrule decisions by judiciary

****

42   House of Lords holds the government to account to make sure it works in the best interest of people. Is this statement true or false?

       A   True

       B   False

****

43 The House of Commons has powers to overrule the House of Lords. Is this statement true or false?

    A   True

    B   False

****

44 Who chairs the debates in the House of Commons?

    A   Prime Minister

    B   Chief Whip

    C   Speaker

    D   Queen

****

45 How is the Speaker selected by other MPs?

    A   By Secret Ballot

    B   By Show of Hands

    C   Online voting

    D   They post their votes to the PM

****

46 Which of the following statements is correct?

    A   If you become a speaker, your constituency will need a by-election to elect another MP

    B   If you become a speaker, you will still continue as an MP of your constituency

****

47 Speaker always represents the ruling party. Is this statement true or false?

    A   True

    B   False

****

48   Speaker makes sure the opposition has a guaranteed amount of time to debate issues. Is this statement true or false?

      A   True

      B   False

****

49   How frequently are general elections held in UK?

      A   Each year

      B   Once in 2 years

      C   Once in 4 years

      D   Once in 5 years

****

50   When are by-elections held?

      A   When prime minister chooses

      B   When an MP dies or resigns

      C   Only on request of Queen

      D   When a 'Life Peer' dies

****

51   MP's are elected through which of these systems in UK?

      A   Proportional representation

      B   First Pass the Post

      C   First kick the post

      D   First knock the post

****

52   In UK, members for European Parliament are elected through which of these systems?

      A   Proportional representation

      B   First Pass the Post

      C   First kick the post

      D   Disproportional representation

****

53   How frequently are elections for European Parliament held in UK?

    A   Each year

    B   Once in 2 years

    C   Once in 4 years

    D   Once in 5 years

****

54   What are elected members for European parliament called?

    A   MPs

    B   MA's

    C   MEPs

    D   AM's

****

55   Contact details of MPs, MEPs & MSPs can be found from which TWO of these resources?

    A   Your local News Agent

    B   BT Phonebook & Yellow Pages

    C   Websites such as www.Parliament.uk

    D   Your local Supermarket

****

56   Who becomes the Prime Minister?

    A   Leader of the Political Party in Power

    B   Leader of the Opposition Party

    C   A life peer

    D   Only a member of Royal family can be a prime minister in UK

** ******

57   Who appoints the members of the cabinet?

    A   The Queen rules if no party wins majority
    B   The Prime Minister
    C   The Chief Whip
    D   The Speaker

****

58   Which of these is the official home of the Prime Minister?

    A   The Buckingham Palace
    B   The Tower of London
    C   10 Downing Street
    D   11, Knightsbridge

** *

59   The Prime Minister also has a country house outside London, called what?

    A   Rural Palace
    B   Chequers
    C   PM House
    D   Squares

****

60   Once formed, Prime Minister cannot be changed for five years. Is this statement true or false?

    A   True
    B   False

****

61   How many senior MPs does the prime minister appoint to become ministers in charge of departments?

    A   20
    B   37
    C   45
    D   10

****

62 **What are the responsibilities of the Chancellor of the Exchequer?**

    A   He looks after the Chequers

    B   He is Chancellor of all the Universities in UK

    C   Responsible for Economy

    D   Responsible for Running of Police Department

****

63 **What are the responsibilities of the Home Secretary?**

    A   Crime & Policing

    B   Education

    C   Immigration

    D   Defence

****

64 **What are the responsibilities of the Foreign Secretary?**

    A   Dealing with unrest in country

    B   Immigration control & Foreign Policy

    C   Managing relationships with foreign countries

    D   Crimes

****

65 **Which of these responsibilities are given to Secretaries of the State?**

    A   Crimes

    B   Defence

    C   Health

    D   Foreign Affairs

****

66   How frequently does the cabinet usually meet?

        A   Annually
        B   Quarterly
        C   Monthly
        D   Weekly

****

67   Which of these is true about decisions made by cabinet?

        A   Cabinet can make decisions that do not have to be
                debated or approved by Parliament
        B   Many of cabinet decisions have to be debated or
                approved by Parliament

****

68   What is the second largest party in the House of
        Commons called?

        A   Opposition
        B   Opposite Wing
        C   Opposite Party
        D   Next ruling party

****

69   Prime Minister Questions are held once per which of
        these?

        A   Year
        B   6 months
        C   Month
        D   Week

****

70   Which MPs are in the Shadow Cabinet?

      A   Opposition Leader

      B   Opposition MPs

      C   Prime Minister

      D   Speaker

****

71   Who selects the Shadow Cabinet?

      A   Members of the Cabinet

      B   House of Commons

      C   Leader of Opposition

      D   Prime Minister

****

72   What is the role of Shadow Cabinet?

      A   To hinder in policies of government

      B   To support government in all matters even when they think its wrong

      C   To challenge the government and put forward alternative policies

      D   To vote against Prime Minister

****

73   Who can stand for elections as an MP?

      A   Anyone aged 18 or over can stand for election as an MP

      B   Anyone aged 21 or over can stand for election as an MP

      C   Anyone aged 30 or over can stand for election as an MP

      D   Only members of big political parties can stand for elections as MP

****

74   It is more likely to win in elections for an MP if you are standing as which of these?

     A   As member of a big political party

     B   As an independent candidate

     C   As a civil servant

     D   As an officer in the Armed forces

****

75   Which TWO of these are the main political parties in UK?

     A   Labour party

     B   Greenpeace party

     C   Conservatives

     D   UKIP

****

76   How frequently do the major parties hold policy making conferences?

     A   Every month

     B   Every Quarter

     C   Every year

     D   Every two years

****

77   What are pressure or lobby groups?

     A   These are organisations which try to influence government policy

     B   They keep pressure on opposition

     C   Government keeps pressure on them

     D   They keep pressure on public

****

78   What do civil servants do?

        A   Join a political party
        B   Carry out government policy
        C   Oppose government policy
        D   Support opposition party

79   Which of these are true about civil servants?

        A   Civil servants are not accountable to ministers
        B   They are politically partial in favour of ruling party
        C   Civil servants support the government in developing and implementing its policies
        D   Civil Servants change every 2 years

80   Towns, cities and rural areas in the UK are governed by which of these?

        A   European Parliament
        B   Councils or Local Authorities
        C   Only central government
        D   Local police

81   An area can have either a district council or a county council, not both. Is this statement true or false?

        A   True
        B   False

82   How are the local authorities funded? Mark TWO correct answers

        A   Local taxes
        B   National Lottery
        C   Funds from Central Government
        D   By wages of local MPs

83   About Mayor, which TWO of these are true?

     A   Mayor is usually a ceremonial leader of council

     B   In some towns mayor is effective leader

     C   MP's are Mayors of their councils

     D   Mayors are Civil Servants

84   How many local authorities are there in London?

     A   33

     B   10

     C   5

     D   55

85   When are the local elections for councillors held in local authorities?

     A   September each year

     B   September every five years

     C   May each year

     D   May, every five years

86   When did UK give some powers to Wales, Scotland and Northern Ireland, over matters that directly affect them?

     A   1914

     B   1947

     C   1970

     D   1997

87 Since when has there been a Welsh Assembly and a Scottish Parliament?

     A   1947

     B   1970

     C   1997

     D   1999

****

88 Which TWO of these powers remain under central government control in UK and not in hands of devolved governments in Wales, Scotland and Northern Ireland?

     A   Policy and laws governing defence & foreign affairs

     B   Policy and laws governing education

     C   Policy and laws governing immigration, taxation and social security

     D   Policy and laws governing health and civil law

****

89 Where is Welsh National Assembly based?

     A   Edinburgh

     B   Glasgow

     C   Cardiff

     D   London

****

90 How many members are there in Welsh Assembly?

     A   50

     B   108

     C   129

     D   60

****

91 How many members are there in Scottish Parliament?

    A   60
    B   129
    C   108
    D   201

****

92 How many members are there in Northern Ireland Assembly?

    A   201
    B   129
    C   60
    D   108

****

93 How often are elections held for Welsh assembly?

    A   Each year
    B   Once in 2 years
    C   Once in 4 years
    D   Once in 5 years

****

94 Members of Welsh Assembly are elected through which of these systems?

    A   Proportional representation
    B   First Pass the Post
    C   First kick the post
    D   Disproportional representation

****

95 Members of Scottish Parliament are elected through which of these systems?

    A   Proportional representation
    B   First Pass the Post
    C   First kick the post
    D   Disproportional representation

****

96   The matters, on which the Scottish Parliament can legislate, include which TWO of these?

      A   Health & Education
      B   Immigration
      C   Civil & Criminal Law
      D   Defence

****

97   A Northern Ireland Parliament was first established in 1922, but abolished later. Is this statement true or false?

      A   True
      B   False

****

98   When was the Northern Ireland Parliament abolished?

      A   1922
      B   1969
      C   1972
      D   1975

****

99   When did Troubles break out in Northern Ireland?

      A   1922
      B   1969
      C   1972
      D   1975

****

100   The Northern Ireland Assembly was established soon after the Belfast Agreement [or Good Friday Agreement] in which year?

      A   1922
      B   1969
      C   1972
      D   1998

****

101   Since which year is Northern Ireland Assembly running successfully without being dissolved?

    A   1970
    B   1998
    C   2007
    D   2012

****

102   The matters, on which the Northern Ireland Assembly can legislate, include which of these?

    A   Health
    B   Education
    C   Civil & Criminal Law
    D   Defence

****

103   How many times has UK government dissolved Northern Ireland Assembly?

    A   Only Once
    B   Twice
    C   Several times
    D   Never

*** *

104   Where is Hansard available?

    A   Large libraries
    B   Internet
    C   Television
    D   Supermarket

****

105   What are the elected members in the Northern Ireland known as?

    A   MEPs

    B   MPs

    C   MLAs

    D   MNAs

****

106   What are the elected members in Scotland known as?

    A   MSAs

    B   MSPs

    C   MEPs

    D   MLAs

****

107   What are the elected members in Wales known as?

    A   PMs

    B   MSPs

    C   MLAs

    D   AMs

****

108   Where do the elected members in Wales meet?

    A   Holyrood, Edinburgh

    B   Senedd, Cardiff

    C   Stormont, Belfast

    D   Westminster, London

****

109   Where do the elected members in Scotland meet?

    A   Westminster, London

    B   Stormont, Belfast

    C   Holyrood, Edinburgh

    D   Senedd, Cardiff

****

110   Where do the elected members in Northern Ireland meet?

> A   Stormont, Belfast
>
> B   Westminster, London
>
> C   Senedd, Cardiff
>
> D   Holyrood, Edinburgh

****

111   Proceedings in Parliament are published in official reports called what?

> A   Hansard
>
> B   Magna Carta
>
> C   Proceedings
>
> D   Charter

****

112   From where do most people get information about political issues and events?

> A   Neighbours
>
> B   Pubs
>
> C   Newspapers, TV, radio & internet
>
> D   Hospitals

****

113   UK has a free press, which means?

> A   All newspapers are free for public
>
> B   Employees work for free for press
>
> C   What is written in newspapers is free from government control
>
> D   All journalists are free lancers

****

114   Newspapers are always impartial and politically neutral. Is this statement true or false?

     A   True
     B   False

****

115   Laws says that opposition party should get more time on radio and TV to express their views. Is this statement true or false?

     A   True
     B   False

****

116   Since when has UK had a fully democratic voting system?

     A   1928
     B   1918
     C   1947
     D   1997

****

117   When was the present voting age set at 18?

     A   1918
     B   1928
     C   1969
     D   1997

****

118   Only UK born citizens have a right to vote. Is this statement true or false?

     A   True
     B   False

*** *****************

119   Which TWO of these groups can vote in all public elections in the UK?

      A   UK citizens

      B   Commonwealth & Irish citizens

      C   European Citizens

      D   US Citizens

****

120   The citizens of EU states who are residents in the UK, can vote in which TWO of these elections?

      A   Elections for European Parliament

      B   Local Authority Elections

      C   General/ National parliamentary elections

      D   By-elections

****

121   What is the register for electors known as?

      A   Voters register

      B   Electoral register

      C   Register for elections

      D   Important register

****

122   You must have your name on the electoral register, for which of these?

      A   To be able to vote in a Parliamentary, local or European election

      B   Only if you are standing for election

      C   If you are opening a bank account

      D   If you are buying a house

****

123   If you are eligible to vote, you can register by contacting which of these?

    A   Your GP

    B   Your local police

    C   Your local council electoral registration office

    D   Your MP

****

124   If you don't know which local authority you come under, you can find out by visiting which of these websites?

    A   www.aboutmyvote.co.uk

    B   www.hmrc.gov.uk

    C   www.ukba.gov.uk

    D   www.nhs.co.uk

****

125   You can only download voter registration forms in English. Is this statement true or false?

    A   True

    B   False

****

126   How frequently is the electoral register updated?

    A   September or October each year

    B   September or October every five years

    C   May each year

    D   May, every five years

****

127   In England, how many electoral registration forms will you expect to receive for your household?

    A   One each for every member of the household

    B   One for the family members and one for the guests

    C   One covering all members of household

    D   None

****

128   System of 'Individual Registration' in which everyone should complete their own form, operates in which part of UK?

    A   Scotland

    B   Wales

    C   England

    D   Northern Ireland

****

129   Which of these is true regarding Electoral register?

    A   Is confidential, should not be available to public

    B   Should be available for everyone to look at, under supervision

****

130   Where can you find an electoral register? Select TWO correct answers.

    A   At local Electoral Registration Office

    B   Some Libraries

    C   Universities

    D   Hospitals

****

131   What are polling stations called in Scotland?

    A   Polling place

    B   Polling booths

    C   Polling centres

    D   Voting centres

****

132 On Election Day, what are the opening times of a polling station?

 A   7 am to 7pm

 B   9 am to 9 pm

 C   10 am to 10 pm

 D   7 am to 10 pm

****

133 While voting, the staff at polling station will give you a ballot paper. How should you fill your ballot paper?

 A   In front of the polling station staff

 B   Privately in a polling booth at polling station

 C   Take the ballot paper to your home and fill it there

 D   It is prefilled, you only need to put it in ballot box without filling

****

134 Who can tell you whom to vote?

 A   No one, only you have the right to make your choice

 B   Your partner can tell you

 C   If you are not sure, polling station staff should tell you whom to vote for

 D   See who the person in front of you is voting

****

135 If you register for postal vote, when do you get your ballot paper?

 A   After election

 B   On day of election

 C   Before election

 D   Never

****

136   Which TWO in this list cannot stand for public office?

   A   Criminals
   B   Doctors
   C   Members of armed forces
   D   General public

****

137   In order for the public to listen to the debates, it is usually easier to get into the House of Lords. Is this statement true or false?

   A   True
   B   False

****

138   Most member states of Commonwealth were once part of the British Empire. Is this statement true or false?

   A   True
   B   False

****

139   How many member states are there in the Commonwealth?

   A   48
   B   52
   C   54
   D   65

****

140   Who is the head of the Commonwealth?

   A   Prime Minister
   B   Queen
   C   Foreign secretary
   D   Commonwealth Union Head

****

141   Commonwealth Law is legally binding on its members. Is this statement true or false?

      A   True

      B   False

****

142   The United Kingdom was one of the countries which formed European Economic Community (EEC). Is this statement true or false?

      A   True

      B   False

****

143   Six countries signed an agreement to make European Union (First named European Economic Community EEC). What was the agreement called?

      A   Magna Carta

      B   Charter of Rights of Six Countries

      C   Treaty of Rome

      D   Hansard

****

144   In which year was EU (Originally named EEC- European Economic Community) formed?

      A   1914

      B   1857

      C   1957

      D   1997

****

145   In which year did UK become a member of European Union?

      A   1957

      B   1973

      C   1997

      D   1999

****

146 **Which of these countries initially formed European Union (or EEC)? Select TWO correct groups.**

    A   France, Italy & Germany

    B   UK, Germany & France

    C   Belgium, Luxembourg & Netherlands

    D   UK, US & France

****

147 **Which of the following statements is correct?**

    A   Croatia will become a member state in 2013

    B   Croatia became a member state in 2012

****

148 **Currently how many EU member states are there?**

    A   20

    B   27

    C   31

    D   35

****

149 **What are EU's powers over its members?**

    A   EU law is legally binding in all its member states, including UK

    B   EU law is legally binding in all the other EU member states, but not in UK

    C   EU has minimal powers over its member states

    D   EU has no powers over its member states

****

150 **What are the European Laws called? Mark TWO correct answers.**

    A   Directives or Regulations

    B   Orders

    C   Framework decisions

    D   Super Orders

****

151   Council of Europe is just another name for European Union. Is this statement true or false?

      A   True

      B   False

****

152   How many member states are there in the Council of Europe?

      A   52

      B   27

      C   102

      D   47

****

153   Which of the following statements is correct?

      A   UK is a member of Council of Europe

      B   UK is not a member of Council of Europe

****

154   What is the Council of Europe responsible for?

      A   Protecting the Environment

      B   World Peace

      C   Protection' and promotion of human rights in member countries

      D   Catching Criminals

****

155   European Convention on Human Rights was drawn by which of these?

      A   Commonwealth

      B   European Union

      C   The Council of Europe

      D   United Nations

****

156 How many member states are there in the United Nations?

    A   27
    B   52
    C   47
    D   190

****

157 What is the United Nations responsible for? Mark TWO correct answers.

    A   Protecting the Environment
    B   Preventing War
    C   Protection and promotion of human rights in member countries
    D   Promoting World Peace

****

158 When was United Nations set up?

    A   After first World War
    B   Before 2nd World War
    C   After 2nd World War
    D   Before First World War

****

159 How many member states are there in Security Council of the United Nations?

    A   15
    B   27
    C   47
    D   52

****

160   How many member of the Security Council are permanent?

A   2

B   3

C   5

D   8

****

161   What does the Security Council do?

A   Recommends action during international crises and threats to peace

B   Protects environment

C   Encourages trade between countries

D   Makes internal policies for member countries

****

162   What is the status of UK's membership in the Security Council?

A   UK is a permanent member

B   UK is a floating member

****

163   What does NATO stand for?

A   North Asian Treaty Organisation

B   North Atlantic Treaty Organisation

C   New Atlantic Treaty Organisation

D   North American Treaty Organisation

****

164   Which of these are members of NATO? Mark TWO correct answers.

A   North America

B   UK & Some European Countries

C   India

D   China

****

165   **Why was NATO set up by member states?**

      A   To help each other in trade and business

      B   To promote human rights

      C   To help each other if they come under attack

      D   To wage war on weaker countries

****

166   **Which of the following statements is correct?**

      A   Those who do not respect the law should not expect to be allowed to become permanent residents in the UK

      B   Those who do not respect law should expect to pay higher application fee to become permanent residents in the UK

****

167   **Which of these is true about Law in the UK?**

      A   Law is different for rich and poor

      B   Law is same for everyone, no matter where they come from or who they are

****

168   **Civil law applies to which TWO of these situations?**

      A   Recovery of debt

      B   Arson

      C   Child Custody issues

      D   Kidnap

****

169   **Which of these is true about law on carrying weapons in UK?**

A   It is ok to carry a knife only for self defence

B   It is ok to carry a knife or a small gun only for self defence

C   It is a criminal offence to carry a weapon of any kind, even if it is for self-defence

D   You can carry any weapon for your security

****

170   **Which of these is true about buying or selling drugs in UK?**

A   You are allowed to buy drugs if you are registered as a licensed drug user

B   You are allowed to sell drugs if you sell in small quantities

C   Both buying or selling drugs such as heroin, cocaine, ecstasy and cannabis is illegal in the UK

D   You can buy any quantity, no restriction is there

****

171   **Which of these is true about law on racial crimes in UK?**

A   It is a criminal offence to cause harassment, alarm or distress due to religion or ethnic origin

B   As far as there is no physical injury, it does not count as offence

C   Racial hatred is unethical but not a crime

D   UK is a free society, you can harass people if you do not like their ethnicity

****

172   **It is illegal in UK to sell tobacco to anyone under what age?**

A   14 years

B   15 years

C   16 years

D   18 years

****

173   **Which of the following statements is correct?**

     A   It is against the law to smoke tobacco products in nearly every enclosed public place in the UK

     B   It is not against the law to smoke tobacco products in public places. You may smoke, if someone minds they will move away.

****

174   **If you are under the legal age limit, you cannot buy alcohol, but an adult can buy for you. Is this statement true or false?**

     A   True

     B   False

****

175   **Drinking in a an alcohol free zone can result in which TWO of these?**

     A   You can easily save yourself by keeping some cash and trying to bribe the police

     B   You can be fined or arrested

     C   It doesn't matter, it is not illegal to drink in alcohol free zones

     D   Police can confiscate alcohol

****

176   **Housing laws address disputes between landlords and tenants regarding which of these?**

     A   Repairs & Evictions

     B   These laws force Landlords to sell houses to tenants

     C   Domestic family issues

     D   Mistreatment of pets

****

177   Consumer rights are related to which of these?

    A   Neighbourhood matters
    B   Traffic incidents
    C   Faulty goods or services
    D   Health issues

****

178   Which of the following statements is correct?

    A   Dispute over wages, unfair dismissal and
         discrimination are covered by Employment laws.
    B   Dispute over wages, unfair dismissal and
         discrimination are not covered by Employment
         laws.

****

179   Which TWO of these are included in the job of the police in UK?

    A   Protect life and property
    B   Act only when crime has happened, and do not
         interfere before that
    C   Prevent and detect crime
    D   Arrange hospital visits for elderly

****

180   Who are police and crime commissioners (PCCS)?

    A   People elected by public to ensure effective local
         police service
    B   Members of House of Lords responsible for
         efficient running of police service
    C   Army Officers
    D   Judges

****

181   When were police and crime commissioners (PCCS) elected?

A   2012

B   2010

C   1997

D   1965

****

182   The police force is a public service that helps and protects only the poor people. Is this statement true or false?

A   True

B   False

****

183   Regarding Police service, which of these is true?

A   Police is allowed to misuse authority in exceptional circumstances

B   Police officers must obey law & must not misuse authority

****

184   Which TWO of these are true regarding police community support officers (PCSOs)?

A   They may have different roles in different areas

B   They usually patrol the streets

C   They always keep guns

D   They arrest violent criminals

****

185   Which of these happens if you are arrested?

A   You will be sent directly to jail

B   You are taken to a   Police station & you are allowed to seek legal advice

C   You will be taken to airport and deported straightaway

D   Nothing, they will just let you go

****

186   Anyone can make a complaint about the police by which TWO of these?

A   By going to a police station

B   By writing to the Chief Constable of the police force involved

C   Talking to your GP

D   Talking to Trading Standards

****

187   Al Qaida and Northern Ireland-related terrorism pose terrorist threats to UK? Is this statement true or false?

A   True

B   False

****

188   Evidence shows that terrorist groups attract very high levels of public support .Is this statement true or false?

A   True

B   False

****

189   If you think someone is trying to persuade you to join an extremist or terrorist cause, what should you do?

A   You should notify your local police force

B   Just ignore them and do not talk to anyone about it

C   Start spying on them without informing anyone

D   Confront them even if it is risky

****

190   Judges or 'the judiciary' are responsible for which of these?

   A   Interpret law & ensure fair trials
   B   Consider applications of asylum seekers
   C   Catch thieves
   D   Find evidence against criminals

****

191   If judges think the actions of government are illegal, what can the government do?

   A   Government has power to ignore judges and override their decisions
   B   Change its policies or ask parliament to change laws
   C   Try to find loopholes in law
   D   Change the judges and ask the new bench to decide

****

192   The government cannot interfere with working of judiciary. Is this statement true or false?

   A   True
   B   False

****

193   Judges also make decisions about contracts, property, employment rights or after an accident. Is this statement true or false?

   A   True
   B   False

****

194 In England, Wales and Northern Ireland, most minor criminal cases are dealt with in which court?

    A   Criminal Courts

    B   Magistrate's Court

    C   Justice of the Peace Court

    D   High Court

****

195 In Scotland, most minor criminal cases are dealt with in which court?

    A   Criminal Courts

    B   Magistrate's Court

    C   Justice of the Peace Court

    D   High Court

****

196 Magistrates and Justices of the Peace (JPs) are members of the House of Lords. Is this statement true or false?

    A   False

    B   True

****

197 Which TWO of these apply to Magistrates and Justices of the Peace (JPs) in England, Wales & Scotland?

    A   They are not paid

    B   They do not need legal qualifications

    C   They are Legally qualified

    D   They have high salaries

** ***********

198   Which of this applies to District Judges or Deputy District Judges in Northern Ireland?

    A   They are not paid

    B   They do not need legal qualifications

    C   They are Legally qualified and paid

    D   They have very high salaries

****

199   In England Wales and Northern Ireland, serious offences are tried in front of which of these?

    A   A judge only in Crown Court

    B   A judge and jury in Crown Court

    C   A jury only in Crown Court

    D   A jury only in civil court

****

200   In Scotland, serious offences are tried in front of which of these?

    A   A Sheriff with a jury in a Sheriff Court

    B   A judge and jury in Crown Court

    C   A jury only in Crown Court

    D   A jury only in civil court

****

201   A jury is made of which of these?

    A   Members of House of Commons

    B   Members of House of Lords

    C   Members of public

    D   Qualified lawyers

****

202   How many members are there in a jury in Scotland?

    A   11
    B   12
    C   15
    D   16

****

203   How many members are there in a jury in England, Wales and Northern Ireland?

    A   11
    B   12
    C   15
    D   21

****

204   When members of public are summoned to do jury service, which TWO of these are true?

    A   It's not mandatory, they can just ignore the summon
    B   They must do it unless they are ill or not eligible
    C   People without proper qualifications are not eligible for jury service
    D   People with a criminal conviction are not eligible for jury service

****

205   When a jury listens to evidence, who gives the verdict of guilty or not guilty?

    A   Jury
    B   Judge
    C   Sheriff
    D   Public

*** ****

206   **When found guilty, who decides the penalty?**

    A   Jury

    B   Judge or Sheriff

    C   Police

    D   Prime Minister

****

207   **Youth courts hear cases when accused persons belong to which age group?**

    A   5 to 15

    B   10 to 17

    C   8 to 18

    D   7 to 17

****

208   **Name or photographs of the accused young person cannot be published in newspapers or used by the media. Is this statement true or false?**

    A   True

    B   False

****

209   **Which of the following statements is correct?**

    A   The parents or carers of the young person are expected to attend the hearing in Youth courts

    B   The parents or careers of the young person are not allowed to attend the hearing in Youth Courts

** ***************

210   **Which system is used in Scotland to deal with children and young people who have committed an offence?**

    A   Youth Conferencing

    B   Young Offenders System

    C   Children's Hearings System

    D   Children's Criminal System

****

211   Which system is used in Northern Ireland to deal with children and young people who have committed an offence?

       A   Youth Conferencing

       B   Young Offenders System

       C   Children's Hearings System

       D   Youth National Rehab System

****

212   What type of cases the County Courts deal with?

       A   Criminal cases

       B   Youth cases

       C   Civil disputes

       D   Child Protection Issues

****

213   Which of these come under jurisdiction of the County Courts?

       A   Family matters, divorces, contracts, Personal injuries & recovering owed money etc

       B   Crimes like murders, big thefts, frauds

****

214   You can use a Small Claims Procedure without help of a lawyer to settle claims in which scenario?

       A   If the claim is less than £5000 in England & Wales

       B   If the claim is less than £5000 in Scotland & Northern Ireland

215   **When do we need a solicitor? Mark TWO correct answers.**

    A   When we need advice on legal matters

    B   When we need to be represented in the court

    C   When we win a lottery

    D   When we open a bank account

216   **In which TWO of these places can you find details of a solicitor if you need one?**

    A   Local Newspapers

    B   Yellow Pages

    C   Local Supermarket

    D   Ask your GP

217   **Which TWO of these are related to protection of individual's rights?**

    A   Hansard

    B   Habeas Corpus Act

    C   Bill of Rights of 1689

    D   Environment Protection Laws

218   **British diplomats played an important role in drafting European Convention on Human Rights. Is this statement true or false?**

    A   True

    B   False

219   When did UK sign European Convention on Human Rights?

       A   1997
       B   1950
       C   1970
       D   2010

****

220   Freedom of expression is recognised as an individual's right in the European Convention on Human Rights. Is this statement true or false?

       A   True
       B   False

****

221   Which TWO of these are recognised as an individual's right in the European Convention on Human Rights?

       A   Right to life
       B   Right to free private medical treatment
       C   Right to a free house
       D   Prohibition of slavery and forced labour

****

222   If you face problems with discrimination based on religion & race etc, you can get more information from which TWO of these?

       A   Citizens Advice Bureau
       B   GP
       C   Equality and Human Rights Commission
       D   No one, you should only contact police

****

223 Regarding domestic violence, which of these can be prosecuted?

    A   Only men, as women are not violent

    B   Anyone, whether they are a man or a woman, married or living together

****

224 A husband cannot be charged with rape of his wife. Is this statement true or false?

    A   False

    B   True

****

225 If you are a victim of domestic violence, which TWO can explain you your options?

    A   GP

    B   Solicitor

    C   Citizens Advice Bureau

    D   Trading Standards

****

226 If you are a victim of domestic violence, what safe places can sometimes be available for you to stay?

    A   Places called Refuges or Shelters

    B   Hospitals

    C   Local Schools

    D   Local Library

****

227 If you are a victim of domestic violence, where would you look for emergency telephone numbers if needed?

    A   Helpline section at the front of Yellow Pages

    B   Your daily paper

****

228   If you are a victim of domestic violence, which TWO can find you a safe place to stay in emergency, if needed?

    A   The 24-hour National Domestic Violence Free phone Helpline

    B   Police

    C   GP

    D   No one can help you

****

229   Female genital Mutilation or cutting is illegal in UK only if done without adequate pain relief. Is this statement true or false?

    A   True

    B   False

****

230   Since Female genital Mutilation is illegal in UK, parents who want it for their girls should take them abroad. Is this statement true or false?

    A   False

    B   True

****

231   Arranged marriages, where both parties agree to the marriage, are acceptable in the UK. Is this statement true or false?

    A   False

    B   True

****

232   Forcing another person to marry is what category of offence?

    A   Minor

    B   Civil

    C   Criminal

    D   Uncategorised

****

233   Forced Marriage Protection Orders were introduced in which year in England, Wales and Northern Ireland?

          A   2008
          B   2002
          C   1997
          D   2012

****

234   Who can apply for the Forced Marriage Protection Orders?

          A   A potential victim
          B   Person who is pressurizing you for marriage
          C   Someone acting on behalf of the victim
          D   Only elder of victim's family

****

235   Self employed do not have to pay tax on their income. Is this statement true or false?

          A   True
          B   False

****

236   Where does the government use the money raised from tax? Mark TWO correct answers.

          A   Big bonuses to MP's
          B   Education
          C   Police & Armed Forces
          D   Bonuses to bankers

****

237 **What is the government department HM Revenue & Customs (HMRC) meant for?**

    A   It is the government department   that collects taxes

    B   Immigration & Customs Issues

    C   Issues National Insurance Numbers

    D   Assesses eligibility for benefits

****

238 **How is the tax paid by most people?**

    A   Deducted directly by their employer from their wages

    B   Most people have to pay their own tax by self assessment

    C   An agent visits monthly to collect taxes

    D   Most people do not pay taxes

****

239 **How does the system of Pay As you Earn (PAYE) work?**

    A   People have to pay their own tax by self assessment, by completing a tax return

    B   Tax is automatically taken by the employer and paid directly to HM Revenue & Customs (HMRC)

    C   People personally go to government departments to pay taxes every year

    D   Employers go to government departments to pay taxes every year

****

240 **On which website can you find out more about income tax?**

    A   Home office's UKBA website.

    B   HMRC Website

    C   Life in the UK Test Website

    D   Local Authority's website

****

241   Who pays National Insurance Contributions (NICs)?

> A   Everyone in paid work
>
> B   Only self employed people
>
> C   Only foreign nationals
>
> D   Only UK citizens

****

242   What is the money raised from National Insurance Contributions used to pay for? Mark TWO correct answers.

> A   Salary of Police
>
> B   State Retirement Pension
>
> C   NHS
>
> D   Salary of Armed forces

****

243   Employees have their National Insurance Contributions deducted from their pay by their employer. Is this statement true or false?

> A   True
>
> B   False

****

244   People who are self-employees do not need to pay National Insurance Contributions. Is this statement true or false?

> A   True
>
> B   False

****

245   If you do not pay enough NICs, what happens?

    A   Nothing, as payments are just voluntary
    B   You will not receive full state retirement pension
         & some benefits
    C   You will be taken to airport and deported
         straightaway
    D   You will be jailed

****

246   Part-time workers, may not qualify for statutory
       payments such as maternity pay if they do no earn
       enough. Is this statement true or false?

    A   True
    B   False

****

247   Many people can share the same National Insurance
       number if they work under same employer. Is this
       statement true or false?

    A   True
    B   False

****

248   Use of National Insurance [NI] number is there to ensure
       you get a good salary. Is this true or false?

    A   False
    B   True

****

249   When do young people receive their National Insurance
       [NI] number?

    A   Just before 12th Birthday
    B   Just before 14th Birthday
    C   Just before 16th Birthday
    D   Just before 18th Birthday

250 A foreign national cannot start work without a National Insurance [NI] number. Is this true or false?

    A   False

    B   True

251 A National Insurance number proves to an employer that you have the right to work in the UK. Is this statement true or false?

    A   False

    B   True

252 Which department issues National Insurance [NI] number?

    A   National Health Service -NHS

    B   HM Revenue & Customs - HMRC

    C   Department for Work and Pensions - DWP

    D   Police

253 To drive a car on public roads in UK, you must be, which of these?

    A   At least 18 year old and have a driving license

    B   At least 16 year old and have a driving license

    C   At least 17 year old

    D   At least 17 year old and have a driving license

254   To get a driving license in UK, you must do, which of these?

  A   Pay the fee to obtain license
  B   Pass the driving test
  C   Know somebody in DVLA
  D   Buy a car

****

255   At what age can you drive a moped?

  A   14
  B   15
  C   16
  D   18

****

256   Your license will be valid till what age initially?

  A   55 years
  B   60 years
  C   67 years
  D   70 years

****

257   After 70 years, you can get a licence for how many years at a time?

  A   2 years
  B   3 years
  C   5 years
  D   10 years

****

258   In Northern Ireland, a newly qualified driver must display which of these, for one year after passing the test?

  A   An R plate (for restricted driver)
  B   A 'P' plate (for Provisional driver)
  C   An 'L' plate (for learner driver)
  D   A 'T' plate (for trainee driver)

****

259 **If your driving license is from a country in the European Union (EU), Iceland. Liechtenstein or Norway, how long can you drive in UK?**

   A   For as long as your license is valid

   B   One year, then get a Full UK driving license

   C   Your license is not valid in UK, you need a Full UK driving license straightaway

   D   Two years at least

****

260 **If your driving license is from a country other than European Union (EU), Iceland. Liechtenstein or Norway, how long can you drive in UK?**

   A   For as long as your license is valid

   B   One year, then get a Full UK driving license

   C   Your license is not valid in UK, you need a Full UK driving license straightaway

   D   5 years at least

****

261 **If you are resident in the UK, your car or motor cycle must be registered at which of these agencies?**

   A   National Health Service -NHS

   B   Your local council

   C   Driver and Vehicle Licensing Agency - DVLA

   D   Department for Work and Pensions - DWP

*** *****

262 **Which of these is true about your Vehicle's Road Tax?**

   A   Pay an Annual Tax & Display the Tax Disc

   B   Pay Tax every 3 years & Display the Tax Disc

   C   Pay Tax every 3 years

   D   Pay Tax every 2 years & Display the Tax Disc

****

263   Insurance is not compulsory if you have a car or a
       motorcycle. Is this statement true or false?

       A   True
       B   False

****

264   Which of these is true regarding driving without a valid
       motor insurance?

       A   It is a minor offence, you will get a caution from
             police
       B   It is not an offence, but it will be expensive for
             you if you have an accident
       C   It is a serious criminal offence
       D   It is a serious criminal offence and you will
             straightaway go to jail

****

265   You have a brand new car. When must your vehicle take
       a Ministry of Transport (MOT) Test?
       A   Each year
       B   Every two years
       C   Every three years
       D   First when it is three year old, then every year

** *

266   Good citizens keep away from party politics and casting
       votes in elections. Is this statement true or false?

       A   True
       B   False

****

267   As a good citizen, when you move to a new place you
       should steer clear of your neighbours, as they might not
       be your type. Is this statement true or false?

       A   False
       B   True

****

268   You can help prevent any problems and conflicts with your neighbours by which TWO of these?

A   Play loud music and keep an eye on their private matters

B   Respect their privacy

C   Avoid noise

D   Watch their activities with a CCTV

****

269   Regarding Refuse Bags & Bins, which of these is true?

A   You should keep them permanently on the street, it is easier that way

B   You should only put your refuse bags and bins on the street if they are due be collected

C   It does not matter what you do, make your own choice

D   If your neighbours are unfriendly, leave your bins close to their side

****

270   How is volunteering and helping your community good for you as a citizen? Mark TWO correct answers.

A   It provides opportunity to develop skills and quickly find a job

B   You may get free stuff

C   It enables you to integrate and get to know other people

D   It wastes time and is not helpful

****

271   How is the jury selected?

A   They look at your bank accounts and select poor people to act as jury

B   They ask people in the audience in courts to come forward and volunteer

C   They ask police to visit homes and choose people

D   Anyone from Electoral register aged 18-70 can be randomly selected

****

272   Parents can often help in classrooms, only if they are themselves qualified teachers. Is this statement true or false?

     A   False
     B   True

****

273   Many schools organise events to raise money for which TWO of these?

     A   To buy extra equipment
     B   To pay bonuses to teachers
     C   For out-of-school activities
     D   To buy clothes for teachers

****

274   Which TWO of these activities schools usually use to raise money?

     A   Sending children to work in a nearby child safe factory
     B   Selling Books & Toys
     C   Selling cooked food
     D   Selling the school building

****

275   School governors in Scotland, are members of which of these?

     A   House of Commons
     B   House of Lords
     C   General public
     D   Parent Teacher Association

****

276 If you are interested in becoming a school governor in England, which TWO of these apply?

    A   Contact your local school

    B   Apply online

    C   Participate in local elections

    D   Talk to your GP

****

277 If you wish to become a school governor, you should be at least how old on the date of election or appointment?

    A   18 year

    B   21 year

    C   35 year

    D   No age bar

****

278 In England, which TWO of these can apply to open a free school in their local area?

    A   MPs only

    B   Parents

    C   Community Groups

    D   Only Teachers

****

279 It is very difficult to join a political party as they are very careful about having new people they do not know. Is this statement true or false?

    A   True

    B   False

****

280   Which of the following statements is correct?

    A   You don't have to tell a canvasser how you intend to vote if you don't want to

    B   It is your duty to tell the canvasser who would you vote for

****

281   Which of these can stand for election as an MP?

    A   European Citizen

    B   Irish Citizens & Commonwealth Citizens

****

282   What are the TWO roles you can play for police as a volunteer?

    A   Chief of police

    B   Special Constable

    C   Lay Non Police representative

    D   Officer In charge of Police station

****

283   For which TWO of these can you volunteer?

    A   Governor of School

    B   Magistrate's Court

    C   For a Hospital, as a nurse, without any prior training

    D   For a Hospital, as a Surgeon, even if you are not qualified

****

284   How long does it take to donate blood?

    A   Only half a day

    B   Only 4 hours

    C   One hour

    D   Full day

****

285 Which TWO of these body tissue/ organs living people can donate?

    A   Blood

    B   Heart

    C   One kidney

    D   A lung

****

286 NSPCC is a charity for which of these?

    A   Children

    B   Older People

    C   Environment

    D   Medical Research

****

287 Age UK is a charity for which of these?

    A   Children

    B   Older People

    C   Homeless

    D   Medical Research

****

288 Crisis is a charity for which of these?

    A   Children

    B   Older People

    C   Homeless

    D   Medical Research

****

289 Cancer Research UK is a charity for Medical research. Is this statement true or false?

    A   True

    B   False

290   **Which of these are charities for environment?**

     A   Shelter

     B   Friends of the Earth

     C   Hope

     D   National Trust

291   **PDSA is a charity for which of these?**

     A   Animals

     B   Older People

     C   Environment

     D   Medical Research

292   **What does PDSA stand for?**

     A   Pale Dying & Sick Animals

     B   People's Dispensary for Sick Animals

293   **Should young people volunteer?**

     A   Yes, they develop their skills through volunteering and receive accreditation

     B   No, they gain nothing, it's just a waste of time.

294   **Who is the National Citizen Service programme for?**

     A   Immigrants

     B   Older People, over 65 years

     C   Young 16-17 year olds

     D   Only for people recently released from prisons

295   Regarding using recycled materials to make new products, which TWO of these is true?

       A   It uses less energy and less rubbish is created

       B   It is unethical, as the formed products are of very poor quality

       C   It means we do not need to extract more raw materials from the earth

       D   Recycling produces toxic gases

****

296   A good way to support your local community is to shop for products from which of these?

       A   Locally if possible

       B   Always go to big supermarkets as there is a huge variety

****

297   How can you reduce your carbon footprint? Mark TWO correct answers.

       A   Buy locally

       B   Prefer driving on walking

       C   Prefer public transport on own car

       D   Shop from distant areas

****

ANSWER KEY

| Q.# | Answer | Reference | |
		Chapter	Page No.
1.	C	The UK government, the law and your role	p. 119
2.	C	The UK government, the law and your role	p. 119
3.	C	The UK government, the law and your role	p. 119
4.	C	The UK government, the law and your role	p. 119
5.	A & B	The UK government, the law and your role	p. 120
6.	A	The UK government, the law and your role	p. 120
7.	D	The UK government, the law and your role	p. 120
8.	B	The UK government, the law and your role	p. 120
9.	A	The UK government, the law and your role	p. 120
10.	B	The UK government, the law and your role	p. 120
11.	A	The UK government, the law and your role	p. 121
12.	B & C	The UK government, the law and your role	p. 121
13.	B	The UK government, the law and your role	p. 121
14.	A	The UK government, the law and your role	p. 121
15.	B	The UK government, the law and your role	p. 121
16.	C	The UK government, the law and your role	p. 122
17.	C	The UK government, the law and your role	p. 122
18.	B	The UK government, the law and your role	p. 122
19.	D	The UK government, the law and your role	p. 122
20.	B & C	The UK government, the law and your role	p. 122
21.	B	The UK government, the law and your role	p. 122
22.	A	The UK government, the law and your role	p. 122

ANSWER KEY

| Q.# | Answer | Reference | |
		Chapter	Page No.
23.	C	The UK government, the law and your role	p. 122
24.	D	The UK government, the law and your role	p. 122
25.	A	The UK government, the law and your role	p. 123
26.	B	The UK government, the law and your role	p. 123
27.	B	The UK government, the law and your role	p. 123
28.	A	The UK government, the law and your role	p. 123
29.	D	The UK government, the law and your role	p. 123
30.	A	The UK government, the law and your role	p. 123 - picture
31.	B	The UK government, the law and your role	p. 124
32.	B	The UK government, the law and your role	p. 124
33.	C	The UK government, the law and your role	p. 124
34.	A & B	The UK government, the law and your role	p. 124
35.	B	The UK government, the law and your role	p. 124
36.	B & C	The UK government, the law and your role	p. 124
37.	A	The UK government, the law and your role	p. 124
38.	A & B	The UK government, the law and your role	p. 124
39.	B	The UK government, the law and your role	p. 124
40.	A	The UK government, the law and your role	p. 125
41.	B & C	The UK government, the law and your role	p. 125
42.	A	The UK government, the law and your role	p. 125
43.	A	The UK government, the law and your role	p. 125

ANSWER KEY

| Q.# | Answer | Reference | |
		Chapter	Page No.
44.	C	The UK government, the law and your role	p. 125
45.	A	The UK government, the law and your role	p. 125
46.	B	The UK government, the law and your role	p. 125
47.	B	The UK government, the law and your role	p. 125
48.	A	The UK government, the law and your role	p. 125
49.	D	The UK government, the law and your role	p. 125
50.	B	The UK government, the law and your role	p. 125
51.	B	The UK government, the law and your role	p. 125
52.	A	The UK government, the law and your role	p. 126
53.	D	The UK government, the law and your role	p. 126
54.	C	The UK government, the law and your role	p. 126
55.	B & C	The UK government, the law and your role	p. 126
56.	A	The UK government, the law and your role	p. 127
57.	B	The UK government, the law and your role	p. 127
58.	C	The UK government, the law and your role	p. 127
59.	B	The UK government, the law and your role	p. 127
60.	B	The UK government, the law and your role	p. 127
61.	A	The UK government, the law and your role	p. 127
62.	C	The UK government, the law and your role	p. 127
63.	A & C	The UK government, the law and your role	p. 127
64.	C	The UK government, the law and your role	p. 127
65.	B & C	The UK government, the law and your role	p. 127

ANSWER KEY

Q.#	Answer	Reference	
		Chapter	Page No.
66.	D	The UK government, the law and your role	p. 127
67.	B	The UK government, the law and your role	p. 127
68.	A	The UK government, the law and your role	p. 127
69.	D	The UK government, the law and your role	p. 128
70.	B	The UK government, the law and your role	p. 128
71.	C	The UK government, the law and your role	p. 128
72.	C	The UK government, the law and your role	p. 128
73.	A	The UK government, the law and your role	p. 128
74.	A	The UK government, the law and your role	p. 128
75.	A & C	The UK government, the law and your role	p. 128
76.	C	The UK government, the law and your role	p. 128
77.	A	The UK government, the law and your role	p. 128
78.	B	The UK government, the law and your role	p. 128
79.	C	The UK government, the law and your role	p. 128
80.	B	The UK government, the law and your role	p. 129
81.	B	The UK government, the law and your role	p. 129
82.	A & C	The UK government, the law and your role	p. 129
83.	A & B	The UK government, the law and your role	p. 129
84.	A	The UK government, the law and your role	p. 129
85.	C	The UK government, the law and your role	p. 129
86.	D	The UK government, the law and your role	p. 129
87.	D	The UK government, the law and your role	p. 129

ANSWER KEY

| Q.# | Answer | Reference | |
		Chapter	Page No.
88.	A & C	The UK government, the law and your role	p. 129
89.	C	The UK government, the law and your role	p. 129
90.	D	The UK government, the law and your role	p. 129
91.	B	The UK government, the law and your role	p. 130
92.	D	The UK government, the law and your role	p. 132
93.	C	The UK government, the law and your role	p. 129
94.	A	The UK government, the law and your role	p. 129
95.	A	The UK government, the law and your role	p. 130
96.	A & C	The UK government, the law and your role	p. 131
97.	A	The UK government, the law and your role	p. 131
98.	C	The UK government, the law and your role	p. 131
99.	B	The UK government, the law and your role	p. 131
100.	D	The UK government, the law and your role	p. 131
101.	C	The UK government, the law and your role	p. 132
102.	A & B	The UK government, the law and your role	p. 132
103.	C	The UK government, the law and your role	p. 132
104.	A & B	The UK government, the law and your role	p. 132
105.	C	The UK government, the law and your role	p. 136
106.	B	The UK government, the law and your role	p. 136
107.	D	The UK government, the law and your role	p. 136
108.	B	The UK government, the law and your role	p. 136
109.	C	The UK government, the law and your role	p. 136

ANSWER KEY

Q.#	Answer	Reference Chapter	Page No.
110.	A	The UK government, the law and your role	p. 136
111.	A	The UK government, the law and your role	p. 132
112.	C	The UK government, the law and your role	p. 133
113.	C	The UK government, the law and your role	p. 133
114.	B	The UK government, the law and your role	p. 133
115.	B	The UK government, the law and your role	p. 133
116.	A	The UK government, the law and your role	p. 133
117.	C	The UK government, the law and your role	p. 133
118.	B	The UK government, the law and your role	p. 133
119.	A & B	The UK government, the law and your role	p. 133
120.	A & B	The UK government, the law and your role	p. 133
121.	B	The UK government, the law and your role	p. 134
122.	A	The UK government, the law and your role	p. 134
123.	C	The UK government, the law and your role	p. 134
124.	A	The UK government, the law and your role	p. 134
125.	B	The UK government, the law and your role	p. 134
126.	A	The UK government, the law and your role	p. 134
127.	C	The UK government, the law and your role	p. 134
128.	D	The UK government, the law and your role	p. 134
129.	B	The UK government, the law and your role	p. 134
130.	A & B	The UK government, the law and your role	p. 134
131.	A	The UK government, the law and your role	p. 134

ANSWER KEY

Q.#	Answer	Reference	
		Chapter	Page No.
132.	D	The UK government, the law and your role	p. 134
133.	B	The UK government, the law and your role	p. 135
134.	A	The UK government, the law and your role	p. 135
135.	C	The UK government, the law and your role	p. 135
136.	A & C	The UK government, the law and your role	p. 135
137.	A	The UK government, the law and your role	p. 135
138.	A	The UK government, the law and your role	p. 137
139.	C	The UK government, the law and your role	p. 137
140.	B	The UK government, the law and your role	p. 137
141.	B	The UK government, the law and your role	p. 137
142.	B	The UK government, the law and your role	p. 138
143.	C	The UK government, the law and your role	p. 138
144.	C	The UK government, the law and your role	p. 138
145.	B	The UK government, the law and your role	p. 138
146.	A & C	The UK government, the law and your role	p. 138
147.	A	The UK government, the law and your role	p. 138
148.	B	The UK government, the law and your role	p. 138
149.	A	The UK government, the law and your role	p. 139
150.	A & C	The UK government, the law and your role	p. 139
151.	B	The UK government, the law and your role	p. 139
152.	D	The UK government, the law and your role	p. 139
153.	A	The UK government, the law and your role	p. 139

ANSWER KEY

Q.#	Answer	Reference	
		Chapter	Page No.
154.	C	The UK government, the law and your role	p. 139
155.	C	The UK government, the law and your role	p. 139
156.	D	The UK government, the law and your role	p. 139
157.	B & D	The UK government, the law and your role	p. 139
158.	C	The UK government, the law and your role	p. 139
159.	A	The UK government, the law and your role	p. 139
160.	C	The UK government, the law and your role	p. 139
161.	A	The UK government, the law and your role	p. 139
162.	A	The UK government, the law and your role	p. 139
163.	B	The UK government, the law and your role	p. 139
164.	A & B	The UK government, the law and your role	p. 139
165.	C	The UK government, the law and your role	p. 139
166.	A	The UK government, the law and your role	p. 139
167.	B	The UK government, the law and your role	p. 140
168.	A & C	The UK government, the law and your role	p. 140
169.	C	The UK government, the law and your role	p. 140
170.	C	The UK government, the law and your role	p. 140
171.	A	The UK government, the law and your role	p. 140
172.	D	The UK government, the law and your role	p. 140
173.	A	The UK government, the law and your role	p. 141
174.	B	The UK government, the law and your role	p. 141
175.	B & D	The UK government, the law and your role	p. 141

ANSWER KEY

Q.#	Answer	Reference	
		Chapter	Page No.
176.	A	The UK government, the law and your role	p. 141
177.	C	The UK government, the law and your role	p. 141
178.	A	The UK government, the law and your role	p. 141
179.	A & C	The UK government, the law and your role	p. 141
180.	A	The UK government, the law and your role	p. 142
181.	A	The UK government, the law and your role	p. 142
182.	B	The UK government, the law and your role	p. 142
183.	B	The UK government, the law and your role	p. 142
184.	A & B	The UK government, the law and your role	p. 143
185.	B	The UK government, the law and your role	p. 143
186.	A & B	The UK government, the law and your role	p. 143
187.	A	The UK government, the law and your role	p. 143
188.	B	The UK government, the law and your role	p. 143
189.	A	The UK government, the law and your role	p. 143
190.	A	The UK government, the law and your role	p. 144
191.	B	The UK government, the law and your role	p. 144
192.	A	The UK government, the law and your role	p. 144
193.	A	The UK government, the law and your role	p. 144
194.	B	The UK government, the law and your role	p. 144
195.	C	The UK government, the law and your role	p. 144
196.	A	The UK government, the law and your role	p. 144
197.	A & B	The UK government, the law and your role	p. 144

ANSWER KEY

Q.#	Answer	Reference	
		Chapter	Page No.
198.	C	The UK government, the law and your role	p. 145
199.	B	The UK government, the law and your role	p. 145
200.	A	The UK government, the law and your role	p. 145
201.	C	The UK government, the law and your role	p. 146
202.	C	The UK government, the law and your role	p. 146
203.	B	The UK government, the law and your role	p. 146
204.	B & D	The UK government, the law and your role	p. 146
205.	A	The UK government, the law and your role	p. 146
206.	B	The UK government, the law and your role	p. 146
207.	B	The UK government, the law and your role	p. 146
208.	A	The UK government, the law and your role	p. 146
209.	A	The UK government, the law and your role	p. 146
210.	C	The UK government, the law and your role	p. 146
211.	A	The UK government, the law and your role	p. 146
212.	C	The UK government, the law and your role	p. 146
213.	A	The UK government, the law and your role	p. 146
214.	A	The UK government, the law and your role	p. 147
215.	A & B	The UK government, the law and your role	p. 147
216.	A & B	The UK government, the law and your role	p. 147
217.	B & C	The UK government, the law and your role	p. 148
218.	A	The UK government, the law and your role	p. 148
219.	B	The UK government, the law and your role	p. 148

ANSWER KEY

Q.#	Answer	Reference	
		Chapter	Page No.
220.	A	The UK government, the law and your role	p. 148
221.	A & D	The UK government, the law and your role	p. 148
222.	A & C	The UK government, the law and your role	p. 149
223.	B	The UK government, the law and your role	p. 149
224.	A	The UK government, the law and your role	p. 149
225.	B & C	The UK government, the law and your role	p. 149
226.	A	The UK government, the law and your role	p. 149
227.	A	The UK government, the law and your role	p. 149
228.	A & B	The UK government, the law and your role	p. 149
229.	B	The UK government, the law and your role	p. 150
230.	A	The UK government, the law and your role	p. 150
231.	B	The UK government, the law and your role	p. 150
232.	C	The UK government, the law and your role	p. 150
233.	A	The UK government, the law and your role	p. 150
234.	A & C	The UK government, the law and your role	p. 150
235.	B	The UK government, the law and your role	p. 150
236.	B & C	The UK government, the law and your role	p. 151
237.	A	The UK government, the law and your role	p. 151
238.	A	The UK government, the law and your role	p. 151
239.	B	The UK government, the law and your role	p. 151
240.	B	The UK government, the law and your role	p. 151
241.	A	The UK government, the law and your role	p. 151

ANSWER KEY

Q.#	Answer	Reference Chapter	Page No.
242.	B & C	The UK government, the law and your role	p. 151
243.	A	The UK government, the law and your role	p. 151
244.	B	The UK government, the law and your role	p. 151
245.	B	The UK government, the law and your role	p. 151
246.	A	The UK government, the law and your role	p. 151
247.	B	The UK government, the law and your role	p. 152
248.	A	The UK government, the law and your role	p. 152
249.	C	The UK government, the law and your role	p. 152
250.	A	The UK government, the law and your role	p. 152
251.	A	The UK government, the law and your role	p. 152
252.	C	The UK government, the law and your role	p. 152
253.	D	The UK government, the law and your role	p. 152
254.	B	The UK government, the law and your role	p. 152
255.	C	The UK government, the law and your role	p. 152
256.	D	The UK government, the law and your role	p. 152
257.	B	The UK government, the law and your role	p. 152
258.	A	The UK government, the law and your role	p. 152
259.	A	The UK government, the law and your role	p. 153
260.	B	The UK government, the law and your role	p. 153
261.	C	The UK government, the law and your role	p. 153
262.	A	The UK government, the law and your role	p. 153
263.	B	The UK government, the law and your role	p. 153

ANSWER KEY

Q.#	Answer	Reference	
		Chapter	Page No.
264.	C	The UK government, the law and your role	p. 153
265.	D	The UK government, the law and your role	p. 153
266.	B	The UK government, the law and your role	p. 154
267.	A	The UK government, the law and your role	p. 154
268.	B & C	The UK government, the law and your role	p. 154
269.	B	The UK government, the law and your role	p. 154
270.	A & C	The UK government, the law and your role	p. 154-55, 158
271.	D	The UK government, the law and your role	p. 155
272.	A	The UK government, the law and your role	p. 156
273.	A & C	The UK government, the law and your role	p. 156
274.	B & C	The UK government, the law and your role	p. 156
275.	C	The UK government, the law and your role	p. 156
276.	A & B	The UK government, the law and your role	p. 156
277.	A	The UK government, the law and your role	p. 156
278.	B & C	The UK government, the law and your role	p. 156
279.	B	The UK government, the law and your role	p. 156
280.	A	The UK government, the law and your role	p. 157
281.	B	The UK government, the law and your role	p. 157
282.	B & C	The UK government, the law and your role	p. 157
283.	A & B	The UK government, the law and your role	p. 157
284.	C	The UK government, the law and your role	p. 157

ANSWER KEY

Q.#	Answer	Reference	
		Chapter	Page No.
285.	A & C	The UK government, the law and your role	p. 158
286.	A	The UK government, the law and your role	p. 159
287.	B	The UK government, the law and your role	p. 159
288.	C	The UK government, the law and your role	p. 159
289.	A	The UK government, the law and your role	p. 159
290.	B & D	The UK government, the law and your role	p. 159
291.	A	The UK government, the law and your role	p. 159
292.	B	The UK government, the law and your role	p. 160
293.	A	The UK government, the law and your role	p. 160
294.	C	The UK government, the law and your role	p. 160
295.	A & C	The UK government, the law and your role	p. 160
296.	A	The UK government, the law and your role	p. 160
297.	A & C	The UK government, the law and your role	p. 160

MOCK TEST 1

For best self assessment, you should aim to do the following test in 45 minutes. In the official test 18 correct answers are a 'Pass'.

Start Time: _____   Finish Time: _____

1   Which TWO of these should you NOT do if you wish to be a permanent resident or citizen of the UK?

    A   Fight with neighbours

    B   Respect other people's religious beliefs

    C   Impose your opinions on others

    D   Be polite

****

2   When will an evidence of English language skills at B1 level of European framework become compulsory to apply for citizenship?

    A   October 2013

    B   July 2013

    C   July 2015

    D   October 2018

****

3   Who led the Roman invasion to Britain in 55BC?

    A   Alexander the Great

    B   Julius Caesar

    C   Emperor Claudius

    D   Hitler

****

4   William the Conqueror was the Duke of Normandy. Is this statement true or false?

    A   True

    B   False

****

5 **With which country did English Kings fight the hundred years war?**

    A   Germany

    B   Scotland

    C   Ireland

    D   France

****

6 **In which year was Magna Carta singed?**

    A   1115

    B   1350

    C   1215

    D   1410

****

7 **Catholics believed in each person's own relationship with God. Is this statement true or false?**

    A   True

    B   False

****

8 **Which of these are true about King Charles I? Mark TWO answers.**

    A   He thought the king was directly appointed by God to rule

    B   He tried to impose a revised prayer book in Scotland that led to serious unrest.

    C   He was very popular in his parliament

    D   He was highly skilled politically

****

9   Who were Huguenots?

      A   German Protestants
      B   French Protestants
      C   Russian Protestants
      D   Irish Protestants

****

10   Until 2013, which emperor has reigned Britain for the longest period of time?

      A   Queen Elizabeth I
      B   Queen Victoria
      C   Queen Elizabeth II
      D   Queen Mary

****

11   In the early 20th Century, Britain was a global super-power. Is this statement true or false?

      A   True
      B   False

****

12   Who wrote 'Romeo & Juliet'?

      A   William Wordsworth
      B   William of Orange
      C   William of Normandy
      D   William Shakespeare

****

13   Which TWO of these are true about Sake Dean Mahomet?

      A   He was born in Scotland
      B   He served in Bengal Army
      C   He introduced Shampooing and curry to Britain
      D   He was a melodious singer

****

14   **Who is often regarded as the founder of modern nursing?**

       A   Emmeline Pankhurst

       B   Dame Helen Mirren

       C   Florence Nightingale

       D   Dame Ellen MacArthur

****

15   **Which TWO of these are British inventions?**

       A   The Harrier Jump Jet

       B   ATM Machine

       C   Ballistic Missile

       D   Diesel Engine

****

16   **Welsh is widely spoken in which of the following regions?**

       A   Ireland

       B   Eastern England

       C   Wales

       D   Highlands

****

17   **Eid al Fitr is celebrated by which of these?**

       A   Muslims

       B   Sikhs

       C   Jews

       D   Hindus

****

18   Which TWO of the following names are paired with their field of expertise?

    A   Mo Farah - Distance Runner - Olympic Gold Medallist

    B   Dame Ellen MacArthur - Sailing

    C   Sir Steve Redgrave - Ice Dancing

    D   Andy Murray - Golf champion

****

19   What is Benjamin Britten [1913 -76] known for? Mark TWO correct answers.

    A   The Canterbury Tales

    B   Writing 'A Young Peron's Guide to the Orchestra'

    C   Founding 'Aldeburgh Festival' in Suffolk

    D   Monty Python's Flying Circus

** *****

20   When was Queen's diamond jubilee?

    A   2006

    B   1998

    C   2012

    D   1947

****

21   When did the hereditary peers lose the automatic right to attend the House of Lords?

    A   1928

    B   1958

    C   1999

    D   2009

****

22   The civil servants have to be politically neutral. Is this statement true or false?

    A   True
    B   False

****

23   What is the legal age limit when you can buy alcohol in UK?

    A   14
    B   16
    C   18
    D   21

****

24   How does the system of Self Assessment work?

    A   People have to pay their own tax by self assessment, by completing a tax return
    B   Tax is automatically taken by the employer and paid directly to HM Revenue & Customs (HMRC)
    C   People personally go to government departments to pay taxes every year
    D   Employers go to government departments to pay taxes every year

****

ANSWER KEY

Q.#	Answer	Reference	
		Chapter	Page No.
1.	A & C	The Values & Principles of the UK	p. 8
2.	A	The Values & Principles of the UK	p. 9
3.	B	A long & illustrious history	p. 17
4.	A	A long & illustrious history	p. 19
5.	D	A long & illustrious history	p. 21
6.	C	A long & illustrious history	p. 22
7.	B	A long & illustrious history	p. 27
8.	A & B	A long & illustrious history	p. 32
9.	B	A long & illustrious history	p. 38
10.	B	A long & illustrious history	p. 47
11.	A	A long & illustrious history	p. 53
12.	D	A long & illustrious history	p. 30
13.	B & C	A long & illustrious history	p. 42
14.	C	A long & illustrious history	p. 49
15.	A & B	A long & illustrious history	p. 65
16.	C	A modern, thriving society	p. 74
17.	A	A modern, thriving society	p. 82
18.	A & B	A modern, thriving society	p. 85-86
19.	B & C	A modern, thriving society	p. 91
20.	C	The UK government, the law and your role	p. 122
21.	C	The UK government, the law and your role	p. 124
22.	A	The UK government, the law and your role	p. 128
23.	C	The UK government, the law and your role	p. 141
24.	A	The UK government, the law and your role	p. 151

MOCK TEST 2

For best self assessment, you should aim to do the following test in 45 minutes. In the official test 18 correct answers are a 'Pass'.

Start Time: _____   Finish Time:_____

1   What does UK offer to its citizens?

      A   1000 pounds per year to all citizens
      B   Freedom from unfair discrimination
      C   Free travel for all
      D   Guaranteed jobs

****

2   Life in the UK test can only be taken in English. Is this statement true or false?

      A   True
      B   False

****

3   When did the Romans succeed in occupying Britain?

      A   Bronze Age
      B   1000 BC
      C   55 BC
      D   AD 43

****

4   What is the other name for Middle ages?

      A   Iron Age
      B   Pre-Modern Age
      C   Medieval period
      D   Modern Age

****

5   In 1348, plague killed one third of population of England. What was the name given to this tragedy?

    A   Plague Deaths

    B   Black Death

    C   Massive Death

    D   Triple Death

****

6   Which TWO of these combined to become one English language?

    A   Norman French

    B   Spanish

    C   Anglo-Saxon

    D   Welsh

****

7   Elizabethan period is known for which of these? Mark TWO answers.

    A   Aviation Industry

    B   Poetry & Drama

    C   William Shakespeare

    D   Black Death

****

8   What were the people who supported king Charles I, as opposed to Parliament, called?

    A   Reporters

    B   Supporters

    C   Cavaliers

    D   Roundheads

****

9   British ships used to take slaves to work at which TWO of these?

    A   Sugar Plantations
    B   Chemical Factories
    C   Salt Mines
    D   Tobacco Plantations

10   What were UK's major exports in 19th century?

    A   Iron, coal and cotton cloth
    B   Tea & Spices
    C   Medicines & Herbs
    D   Cars

11   War of Allied forces with Germany ended in which year?

    A   1980
    B   2003
    C   1945
    D   1947

12   Who wrote 'Midsummer Night's Dream'?

    A   William Congreve
    B   Samuel Johnson
    C   William Shakespeare
    D   Robert Burns

13   Act of Union (Ireland) took place in year 1800 and Ireland unified with Great Britain in 1801. Is this statement true or false?
    A   True
    B   False

14 Whose famous statement was this 'I have nothing to offer but blood, toil, tears and sweat'?

    A   Winston Churchill

    B   Margaret Thatcher

    C   Robinhood

    D   Tony Blair

15 Who wrote 'George's Marvellous Medicine'?

    A   Rudyard Kipling

    B   George Eliot

    C   William Blake

    D   Roald Dahl

16 What proportion of the workforce do women make?

    A   A quarter

    B   A third

    C   About half

    D   One fifth

17 On April fool's day, people play jokes on each other until which of these?

    A   Mid-day

    B   End of Week

    C   Until midnight

    D   Until end of the month

18   Both types of rugby have separate leagues and national teams in England, Wales, Scotland and Northern Ireland. Is this statement true or false?

      A   True
      B   False

****

19   Which of the following statements is correct?

      A   People under the legal age of 18 are not allowed in any pub
      B   Under age people (less than 18) may be allowed in some pubs with an adult

****

20   What is the system of government in the UK?

      A   Presidential democracy
      B   Direct democracy
      C   Parliamentary democracy
      D   Dictatorship

****

21   Who keeps order during political debates in the parliament?

      A   Prime Minister
      B   Chief Whip
      C   Speaker
      D   Queen

****

22   The United Kingdom was one of the six countries who formed European Economic Community (EEC). Is this statement true or false?
      A   True
      B   False

****

23   **Which of the following statements is correct?**

         A   The police are organized into a number of separate police forces headed by Chancellor of Exchequer

         B   Police department works without direct control of the government

****

24   **Further guidance about National Insurance Contributions is available on which department's website?**

         A   Home office's UKBA website.

         B   HMRC Website

         C   Life in the UK Test Website

         D   Local Authority's website

****

ANSWER KEY

Q.#	Answer	Reference	
		Chapter	Page No.
1.	B	The Values & Principles of the UK	p. 8
2.	B	The Values & Principles of the UK	p. 10
3.	D	A long & illustrious history	p. 17
4.	C	A long & illustrious history	p. 21
5.	B	A long & illustrious history	p. 22
6.	A & C	A long & illustrious history	p. 23
7.	B & C	A long & illustrious history	p. 30
8.	C	A long & illustrious history	p. 33
9.	A & D	A long & illustrious history	p. 43
10.	A	A long & illustrious history	p. 48
11.	C	A long & illustrious history	p. 59
12.	C	A long & illustrious history	p. 30
13.	A	A long & illustrious history	p. 45
14.	A	A long & illustrious history	p. 56
15.	D	A long & illustrious history	p. 68
16.	C	A modern, thriving society	p. 75
17.	A	A modern, thriving society	p. 82
18.	A	A modern, thriving society	p. 88
19.	B	A modern, thriving society	p. 106
20.	C	The UK government, the law and your role	p. 123
21.	C	The UK government, the law and your role	p. 125
22.	B	The UK government, the law and your role	p. 138
23.	B	The UK government, the law and your role	p. 141
24.	B	The UK government, the law and your role	p. 151

MOCK TEST 3

- -

For best self assessment, you should aim to do the following test in 45 minutes. In the official test 18 correct answers are a 'Pass'.

Start Time: _____   Finish Time:_____

1   Which TWO does UK offer to its citizens?

        A   A right to fair trial
        B   Freedom from unfair discrimination
        C   Free lunch at work
        D   Weekly citizenship workshops

****

2   The best preserved prehistoric village of Northern Europe is located in which of these places?

        A   Cornwall in East of England
        B   North of Scotland
        C   Northern Ireland
        D   South Wales

****

3   What was the name of the wall in the north of England to keep out the Picts (ancestors of the Scottish people)?

        A   The Great Wall
        B   The Monument
        C   The Hadrian Wall
        D   Stonehenge

****

4   Who introduced Statute of Rhuddlan that annexed Wales to England?
        A   William the Conqueror
        B   King Edward I
        C   King James II
        D   Queen Mary

****

5   The country needed more food and more cereal crops after plague. Is this statement true or false?

  A   False
  B   True

****

6   Geoffrey Chaucer wrote a series of poems in English about a group of people going to which of these?

  A   Canterbury on a pilgrimage
  B   Canterbury on a War
  C   Cambridge on a pilgrimage
  D   Cambridge on a War

****

7   Sir Francis Drake's ship, was one of the first to sail right around ('circumnavigate') the world. What was its name?

  A   The Golden Hind
  B   Titanic
  C   Venus
  D   Thunder Child

****

8   King Charles II said he had 'no wish to go on his travels again'. What was he referring to?

  A   His passion for hunting
  B   His experience of escape to Europe
  C   He plans to explore the deserts
  D   He had wanted to go for pilgrimages

****

9   William Wilberforce is known for his role in fighting for which of these?

      A   Women's rights

      B   Anti-slavery laws

      C   Child protection laws

      D   Immigration Laws

10   When did Ireland suffer famine?

      A   17th century

      B   18th century

      C   19th century

      D   20th century

11   How many countries first got together to make the European Economic Community?

      A   27

      B   6

      C   53

      D   200

12   Who discovered and wrote about gravity?

      A   Aristotle

      B   Graham Bell

      C   Isaac Newton

      D   Alexander Fleming

13   UK Flag bears crosses of which of these patron saints?

      A   St George of England

      B   Patron Saints of England, Scotland & Ireland

14   Whose famous words are these 'We shall fight on the beaches, we shall fight on the landing grounds..'?

       A   William the Conqueror

       B   St Patrick

       C   Winston Churchill

       D   William Shakespeare

15   Which of the following statements is correct?

       A   Newport is a city in Wales

       B   Newport is a small village in Wales

       C   Newport is a city in Scotland

       D   Newport is a city in Northern Ireland

16   Which of the following statements is correct?

       A   St David is the patron saint of Ireland

       B   St Andrew is the patron saint of Ireland

17   People wear poppies (the red flower found on the battlefields of the First World War) in celebration of which day?

       A   Bonfire Night

       B   Thanksgiving day

       C   Remembrance day

       D   D day

18   Which is the most famous tennis tournament hosted in Britain?

    A   Super League

    B   Six Nations Championship

    C   The Wimbledon Championships

    D   Royal Ascot

****

19   Which TWO of these are the charities to preserve important buildings, coastline and countryside in the UK?

    A   RSPCA

    B   The National Trust in England

    C   National Trust for Scotland

    D   Red Cross

****

20   Queen does not have any important role in government. Is this statement true or false?

    A   True

    B   False

****

21   How can you contact your MPs? Select TWO correct answers.

    A   By Letter

    B   By Telephone

    C   At their home

    D   During Sessions of Parliament

****

22   When did UK become a member of EU?

        A   1914
        B   1957
        C   1973
        D   1997

****

23   Members of the public are allowed in Youth Courts. Is this
        statement true or false?

        A   True
        B   False

****

24   Parents can join Parent Teacher Associations (PTAs), only
        if they are themselves qualified teachers. Is this
        statement true or false?

        A   True
        B   False

****

ANSWER KEY

Q.#	Answer	Reference	
		Chapter	Page No.
1.	A & B	The Values & Principles of the UK	p. 8
2.	B	A long & illustrious history	p. 15
3.	C	A long & illustrious history	p. 17
4.	B	A long & illustrious history	p. 21
5.	A	A long & illustrious history	p. 22
6.	A	A long & illustrious history	p. 23
7.	A	A long & illustrious history	p. 30
8.	B	A long & illustrious history	p. 34
9.	B	A long & illustrious history	p. 43
10.	C	A long & illustrious history	p. 49
11.	B	A long & illustrious history	p. 66
12.	C	A long & illustrious history	p. 35
13.	B	A long & illustrious history	p. 45
14.	C	A long & illustrious history	p. 56
15.	A	A modern, thriving society	p. 72
16.	B	A modern, thriving society	p. 77
17.	C	A modern, thriving society	p. 83
18.	C	A modern, thriving society	p. 89
19.	B & C	A modern, thriving society	p. 107
20.	B	The UK government, the law and your role	p. 122
21.	A & B	The UK government, the law and your role	p. 126
22.	C	The UK government, the law and your role	p. 138
23.	B	The UK government, the law and your role	p. 146
24.	B	The UK government, the law and your role	p. 156

MOCK TEST 4

For best self assessment, you should aim to do the following test in 45 minutes. In the official test 18 correct answers are a 'Pass'.

Start Time: _____   Finish Time:_____

1   The Life in the UK Test questions require an understanding of the English language ESOL Entry level 3. Is this statement true or false?

        A   True
        B   False

****

2   In which age, people learned to make tools and weapons from iron?

        A   Stone Age
        B   Bronze Age
        C   Iron Age
        D   None of these

****

3   Hadrian wall is a UNESCO's World Heritage Site.   Is this statement true or false?

        A   True
        B   False

****

4   What was the name of the Scottish leader who defeated English in Middle Ages?

        A   Robert the Bruce
        B   Robert Wallace
        C   Robert Burns
        D   Robinhood

****

5   **What did Magna Carta do?**

    A   Help king collect taxes
    B   Restrict king from travelling
    C   Restrict king to make changes in law
    D   End Monarchy

****

6   **Henry VIII was most famous for what?**

    A   Courage & Crusades
    B   Love with religion & Spirituality
    C   Wealth and honour
    D   Marriages & breaking away from Church of Rome

****

7   **Charles I believed in divine rights of common men. Is this statement true or false?**

    A   True
    B   False

****

8   **Why was the take over by William of Orange called 'The Glorious Revolution'?**

    A   Because William came with a roar crushing everyone on the way
    B   Because there was no resistance & no fighting in England
    C   Because it guaranteed the power of parliament
    D   Because they looted treasures on their way

****

9 Wellington, who defeated Napoleon, was also known as which of these?

    A   Iron Duke

    B   Wellington the Conqueror

    C   The Conqueror

    D   The Iron Man

10 Regarding Irish nationalist movement, what was Fenians' demand?

    A   Complete Independence for Ireland

    B   Home Rule, in which Ireland would remain in the UK but have its own parliament

11 What did Lady Margaret Thatcher do to the industries?

    A   Privatized Industries

    B   Nationalized Industries

12 Richard Arkwright is remembered as an expert in which of these?

    A   Making Cars

    B   Running Factories

    C   Banking

    D   Hair dressing

13 Who was Florence Nightingale?

    A   A great British actress

    B   Poetess

    C   A nurse

    D   Writer of Harry Potter

****

14   Which TWO of these was William Beveridge known for?

A   The Education Act
B   Economic Reforms
C   The Beveridge Report
D   Discovering Insulin

****

15   Which of the following statements is correct?

A   Northern Ireland & Scotland have their own notes, valid everywhere in the UK, however, shops and businesses do not have to accept them.
B   Northern Ireland & Scotland have their own notes, valid everywhere in the UK, and shops and businesses should by law accept them.

****

16   Which festival is often called 'Festival of lights'?

A   Easter
B   Christmas
C   Hannukah
D   Diwali

****

17   Which TWO of the following names are paired with their achievement?

A   Sir Roger Bannister - first man in the world who ran a mile in less than 4 minutes
B   Sir Jackie Stewart -Captained England Football team
C   Bobby Moore - Played James Bond
D   Sir Ian Botham- captained England Cricket team

****

18   What is the Classical Musical event organised in London by BBC since 1927, called?

        A   Proms
        B   Opera
        C   Les Miserable's
        D   Pomps

****

19   The United Kingdom is a Parliamentary democracy. Is this statement true or false?

        A   True
        B   False

****

20   Why is the House of Commons more important than the House of Lords?

        A   Because House of Commons are more in number
        B   Because public does not like lords
        C   Because they are democratically elected
        D   Because they are easier to reach

****

21   Who approves the important decisions made by the Cabinet?

        A   House of Commons
        B   House of Lords
        C   Parliament
        D   Queen

****

22   Criminal law applies to which TWO of these situations?

      A   Insurance fraud
      B   Kidnap
      C   Murder
      D   Child Custody

****

23   Right to fair trial is recognised as an individual's right in the European Convention on Human Rights. Is this statement true or false?

      A   True
      B   False

****

24   Friends of Earth is a charity for which of these?

      A   Animals
      B   Older People
      C   Environment
      D   Medical Research

****

ANSWER KEY

Q.#	Answer	Reference	
		Chapter	Page No.
1.	A	The Values & Principles of the UK	p. 9
2.	C	A long & illustrious history	p. 16
3.	A	A long & illustrious history	p. 17
4.	A	A long & illustrious history	p. 21
5.	C	A long & illustrious history	p. 22
6.	D	A long & illustrious history	p. 26
7.	B	A long & illustrious history	p. 32
8.	B & C	A long & illustrious history	p. 36
9.	A	A long & illustrious history	p. 44
10.	A	A long & illustrious history	p. 50
11.	A	A long & illustrious history	p. 67
12.	B	A long & illustrious history	p. 41
13.	C	A long & illustrious history	p. 49
14.	B & C	A long & illustrious history	p. 62
15.	A	A modern, thriving society	p. 74
16.	D	A modern, thriving society	p. 81
17.	A & D	A modern, thriving society	p. 85
18.	A	A modern, thriving society	p. 90
19.	A	The UK government, the law and your role	p. 119
20.	C	The UK government, the law and your role	p. 124
21.	C	The UK government, the law and your role	p. 127
22.	B & C	The UK government, the law and your role	p. 140
23.	A	The UK government, the law and your role	p. 148
24.	C	The UK government, the law and your role	p. 159